Wendy Grant has had an extremely varied career including engineering, teaching, parenting a large family, working with animals and managing a family business. She is qualified as a member of the Academy of Applied Psychology and The National Association of Counsellors, Hypnotherapists and Psychotherapists, and was accepted as an accredited member of the Hypnotherapy Register in 1993.

by the same author

Are You In Control?
Dare!
13 to 19

Resolving Conflicts

HOW TO TURN CONFLICT INTO CO-OPERATION

Wendy Grant

ELEMENT
Shaftesbury, Dorset • Rockport, Massachusetts
Melbourne, Victoria

© Element Books Limited 1997
Text © Wendy Grant 1997

First published in Great Britain in 1997 by
Element Books Limited
Shaftesbury, Dorset SP 7 8BP

Published in the USA in 1997 by
Element Books, Inc.
PO Box 830, Rockport, MA 01966

Published in Australia in 1997 by
Element Books Limited
and distributed by Penguin Australia Limited
487 Maroondah Highway, Ringwood, Victoria 3134

Page design by Roger Lightfoot
Illustrations by Alison Campbell
Cover design by Mark Slader
Typeset by Footnote Graphics, Warminster
Printed and bound in Great Britain by J. W. Arrowsmith, Bristol

British Library Cataloguing in Publication
Data available

Library of Congress Cataloging in Publication
Data available

ISBN 1–86204–126–1

Contents

This book is dedicated to those who seek peace and a deeper understanding of themselves and their fellow beings.

Acknowledgements

I wish to thank those who have helped to make this book possible by sharing with me their thoughts and experiences, also for giving their time to answer the many questions asked. We learned a lot from each other and discovered new truths about ourselves we had not known were there. I believe that these insights, if we heed them, will help to make us into better people.

My thanks also to Tom, Simeon and my two sons, Simon and Steve for helpful comments and constructive criticism. You all helped to make the task easier and sometimes even fun.

Note: Where case histories, stories and examples have been used, names, locations and personal details have been changed to protect the confidentiality of those people concerned.

Preface

To benefit fully from this book the reader is advised to begin at the beginning and to read systematically through to the end. Although there is the temptation to delve into the chapter that seems relevant to one's individual needs, points covered in one area may also apply in other situations and so could be overlooked. For example, defensive behaviour dealt with in a workshop environment will apply equally with relatives, friends and strangers; dealing with unfair accusations will apply in all relationships and circumstances. You may not go out to work but will still, at times, enter into a workplace when, for instance, you take your car to be serviced or shop in a superstore – there you interact with staff and for the time you are there you become part of the working environment.

Although you may possibly no longer have any immediate family, you once belonged to one (even if this was an institutional 'family'), and the things that you experienced will have influenced the way you see life and how you cope with it. It is, therefore, important not to skip any of the information and help offered in 'Family Conflicts'.

The instructions given in this book are simple and free from any technical jargon so that you do not need to be a psychologist in order to benefit from reading it. Approach the contents with an open mind, enjoy the experience, have fun, and if you gain one tenth of the insight from reading the book that I have done in writing it, you will have begun your journey into a new way of looking at life and coping with conflict.

Note: In my writing you will notice that I have alternated between the sexes – where this occurs the content applies equally to both (or either); where what I say refers specifically to one gender, it is obvious. Where I have used the plural 'parents' the content does, in many instances, apply also to one parent (or one-parent families).

Introduction

It's 2 o'clock in the morning. I've been sitting in the kitchen beside the Aga stove drinking coffee and thumbing through this week's copy of the *TV Times*. There's nothing odd about that for when my brain's busy I don't sleep much and often end up in the kitchen in the silent hours of the night. But this occasion *is* different. It started five days ago when I awoke with the title for a new book in my head: *Resolving Conflicts*. Just that. Nothing else, no forethought, intent or design. I was curious, alerted. Where did it come from and what was I supposed to write? Was my unconscious mind trying to get a message through to me? I wondered. Although it felt important, I did nothing for two more days. I just let it brew. On the morning of the third day, I saw, amongst the mail lying on the door mat beneath the letter box, a brochure with the words, **How to Manage Conflict**, in large print on the back page.

Well, I don't believe in coincidences. To me it seemed that messages were appearing as if some invisible force was involved. Yet still I did nothing, it was as if I needed one more thing to convince me that I really had to write this book. It came a few minutes ago. On one page of the television magazine I had been idly perusing, my attention was drawn to the picture of a group of people, their backs to the camera as they watched their homes and land being burned. The caption beneath this picture tells of a film to be shown later this week, described as '*a powerful parable of the madness and horror of war*'.

I then acknowledged that for weeks I have been almost overwhelmed by the news of wars between people who shared the same country – the same land. People who were neighbours, some even friends, being terrorized in the most appalling situations. At moments like this I have felt a kind of desperate hopelessness: what can anyone do to turn around these situations or resolve such conflicts?

Now I see clearly that *I* can do something – *that we all can*! To stop war we have to resolve conflicts, not at a national or international level, but between family, friends, neighbours, colleagues and students. There is no way to prevent national or international conflict until we first learn a new way of living that creates harmony, compassion, understanding and caring. It starts at home! How can we expect nations to live in peace when we haven't yet learned to create harmony within our own homes and on our own doorsteps?

I have had plenty of time and opportunities in my life to observe small children and babies and I know that so long as they can have everything the way they want it, there is no conflict. But when you start to say 'No', to restrict and control, you quickly discover that sweet little baby has a very powerful urge to have things his own way. He has yet to learn to live within the structure of a family and a society. If these lessons are not well learned, life becomes intolerable for all those concerned. This principle applies at every level. By learning how to resolve personal conflict, *you* can help change the world.

It is said that there is a 'principle of attraction' that affects all matter: if 17 per cent of anything moves into a changed state the rest will follow. If 17 per cent of water in a pond turns to ice, the rest will attempt to change its state to become ice. If 17 per cent of a group of people are motivated to create good, the rest will be influenced by the actions of those people. The abolition of slavery, women being allowed to vote, the right of all children to be educated and more recently the collapse of communist control in several European countries are a few examples of how this has worked. Until you try, you can have no idea just how effective will be your contribution, or how resolving conflicts within and without will transform your own life.

We have also to learn to live in harmony with Earth. Time is running out. According to physicists and scientists we have about 20 years to turn things around. If we fail, life on Earth will

We have to communicate our needs

disappear as it did many thousands of years ago. Changing from conflict to co-operation is, in fact, all any of us can do to create a stable planet – certainly pollution, nuclear experiments and the destruction of trees has to stop.

You have nothing to lose and everything to gain by helping create positive change. As you read through this book please put the principles and exercises into practice; they are simple, powerful, and will bring you great joy and peace.

This is my promise to you.

WENDY GRANT

1 Thinking Patterns and Processes

Let us start with an experiment. Imagine for a few minutes that someone you trust has agreed to accompany you to an important meeting. This could be your husband attending your son's school concert with you; your mother going with you to the doctor; a colleague helping you present a new project to management. Perhaps you can recall such an occasion from the past.

It's happening tonight. The person concerned is going to be away all day but has faithfully promised to return in time to go with you.

Already it's getting late and you are beginning to feel uptight. Surely he knows how important this is? He has promised – so where is he? The phone rings: *Sorry, I've been delayed. I met a friend I haven't seen for years. He needed a witness to his signature so I went along to the solicitor's office with him. It took ages. Twice the solicitor was called away. I'm really sorry, but I'm just not going to make it.* The phone goes dead.

How do you feel? Angry? Put-out? Furious? Upset? Hurt? Let down? This person, whom you trusted, has failed to keep his promise. He's put his friend first, totally disregarding your feelings.

As you think through the situation, you begin to build up all the resentment such a lack of consideration seems to justify. You may even drag up other past thoughtless actions or omissions. You feel he should be punished. Perhaps you're already planning retribution, some way to make him realize that he can't treat you like this. You would never have done such a thing to him! But now you think – why not turn the tables and do something like this to him tomorrow. Let him find out how it feels! You could decide not to speak to him for a week; you may decide never to trust him again or to believe anything he says. Taken to extremes, you may decide never to trust anyone again. Of course you realize that he may be feeling really bad about the situation – and so he should!

How does this conflict make you feel? Do you experience deep satisfaction at the thought of getting your own back, or making him feel bad? Do you experience a glow of self-righteousness? After all, he deserves all that's coming to him, doesn't he?

Now ask yourself the following questions: *Does my reaction enable me to feel good about the situation? It is productive, rewarding or fulfilling? Will it improve things in the future?*

The answer has to be 'No'. We cannot feel good while we harbour such negative thoughts and feelings.

Let us now try a different way of managing the situation. There's no way of changing it and you can't avoid it. You could make excuses for his thoughtless behaviour but you know in your heart that isn't really going to work. Let us try forgiveness, not in a self-righteous way or by playing the role of martyr, but because you want the best outcome possible from this situation. You can still express your disappointment, or hurt, and allow yourself to be comforted or reassured. He really hadn't intended to get caught up in his friend's problems to the extent that it caused him to be late. A hug, kind words, a tolerant smile can go a long way towards helping you both feel good again.

If this person in your life is always being late or letting you down and you truly care about each other, then you need to take the time to *really communicate your feelings*. Some people do have a struggle to get anywhere on time and then there are others who always get there far too early. I've had both as clients, aware that they have a problem, really wanting to change and not knowing how (*see* Chapter Six).

Taking the scenario described above, and realizing that this person cannot change, do you care enough to accept him as he is – including faults he honestly seems unable to do anything about? If he truly can't change or doesn't want to, then you may have to change your responses to him because punishment and conflict do nothing positive to improve the situation or relationship.

Lack of consideration causes a lot of conflict, from children who leave the house constantly in a mess, to partners who seem always to be doing something that irritates or annoys. Pause, and for a few minutes imagine the house clean and tidy with no noise and no children . . . No hugs or love or fun with them either! Perhaps you can now begin to see the mess as part of those rascals you adore. This doesn't mean you stop trying to teach them to be tidy, but you look for better ways to train and encourage them that avoid conflicts and rows. When you consider the partner who irritates, imagine life without ever having him there to share your thoughts and feelings – no jokes, no laughter, no acts of loving care. Is the emptiness you would be left with really compensation for no frustration or irritation?

As to the person who persistently turns up late – imagine life if they never returned at all. Most of us who have lost someone very close to us wish we had the chance to say and do things differently.

There are always at least two points of view in a conflict. To better manage our lives we need to learn to *listen actively* and be prepared to consider the other person's point of view. This leads naturally to a more tolerant, open-minded road to communication.

I recall a schoolteacher who never ever gave any child the opportunity to explain why he or she had arrived late, or failed to complete their homework, or made a mistake. We were always seen to be in the wrong; it never occurred to him that he could have failed to make himself clear, or that the school bus had been delayed, or that the mistake was part of being human, or caused through fear. He was actively disliked and lacked respect from children and staff alike.

Fortunately we also had a sports mistress who was gentle, compassionate, courteous, and who always took the time to listen to our side of the story. No one was ever intentionally late for her classes and when we heard that she was to be married we carried her shoulder high through the school.

All our behaviour is influenced by conditioning, experiences, beliefs, other people's values, and the thinking patterns and processes we use. By understanding your own thinking processes, and those of others, you can learn to avoid many conflicts, divert disaster and channel the forces of anger into wholesome positive action. You can learn to recognize when you are using blame and do something constructive about it; avoid confrontation when it is wisest to do so; prevent disagreements escalating into rows.

Understanding is the beginning to taking control, both of yourself and situations. Using your strongest points you will not only become successful, likeable, influential, but you will also have the power to make positive changes that will influence all mankind. Remember the 17 per cent rule!

THE WAY WE THINK

The way we think is determined by our genes, personality, and experiences that start in childhood. Depending on our environment, the behaviour pattern of our parents, their response to us, and how our responses are met, we learn to think in certain ways that eventually determine the way we view life and how we deal with it.

Most of us like to think we know ourselves; it is then quite surprising, when we are put through an assessment programme, to discover that for years we have failed to recognize many of our strengths and weaknesses.

I have a friend who never saw herself as able to do anything more than menial jobs which, in reality, failed to utilize her greatest strengths. For some time I had observed how well she organized things such as the school outing, a raffle to raise funds, a charity walk, and I once tried pointing this out to her. 'But that's different!' she protested. 'Someone had to do it, so I just got on and did the best I could.' She completely failed to see that those natural skills could be used to earn a living. Her strengths were in being efficient, practical, highly motivated, and in persuading people rather than pushing them into doing things. But she believed that in order to take charge, one had to be bossy and able to order people about and she knew she was no good at that.

It is helpful, when attempting to understand the thinking patterns most used by yourself and others, to identify the patterns by placing them in groups. (This doesn't mean labelling them and then proceeding with a fixed mind.) When we begin to group thinking patterns and processes, we discover that some people have a strong realistic way of looking at things, others use an analytical approach, then there are the practical ones who need to test out ideas and theories based on their personal experiences, while others like to combine ideas and situations synthesizing these into a complex whole wherever possible. And then, of course, there are the idealists who want everything to be good and right for everyone.

In the following paragraphs I have listed the various attributes, strengths and weaknesses in the five most recognizable ways in which people think. For many of us, our thinking processes are a combination of two or more of these which makes life bearable for us (and others) and gives us a balanced approach to life and its problems. However, there is often a strong tendency towards one in particular which can make communication difficult and lead to frequent conflict. As you read of the various 'types', you should begin to recognize yourself, and others whom you know well.

You may like to pause here and complete the following questionnaire. Doing this now will ensure that your answers are not influenced by having first read the various thinking strategies listed below.

Note: These are not in any order of preference, nor is one more important than another.

THINKING ASSESSMENT QUESTIONNAIRE

Choose one of the five options given for each question and indicate your choice by placing a tick beside it. When you have completed this by systematically working through the set of questions, transfer scores to the chart allowing a score of 5 for each one that you ticked. For example, if you ticked option c in questions 1 you will see beside this the letter **P**, you then place 5 in the column headed with the letter **P**. If you choose option e for question 2 you would then write 5 in the column **S**. When you have done this with all the questions, add up your subtotals in the next box. You can now see your final assessment by transferring these numbers to the box which indicates the various thinking strategies.

If amongst the options there are those to which you will want to give equal weight – don't worry, as previously stated, most of us tend to have a fairly even balance between two main thinking strategies, so just tick one of them.

1 Do you think that in a conflicting situation:
   a. people's feelings matter most
   b. one should focus on the facts
   c. the best thing is to try and bring it to an end as quickly as possible
   d. people can benefit from argument
   e. arguments are rarely satisfactorily resolved

2 When you read a newspaper report do you tend to:
   a. try to verify the facts
   b. believe what you read
   c. believe it if it supports what you know
   d. recognize that reports are biased and make allowances
   e. speculate on the effects of the report

3 Would you prefer to work in:
   a. sales and marketing
   b. creative design and development

   c. adult education and advice
   d. caring and health
   e. accountancy and finance

4 When you read a newspaper or magazine do you first:
   a. read the current news on world affairs
   b. pick out the headlines that interest you
   c. work systematically through from the beginning
   d. read the stories with human interest
   e. choose to read curious stories which reveal new insights

5 When you buy presents for adults do you tend to choose:
   a. something that appeals to you
   b. something you believe the other person will like
   c. the first thing you see that will do
   d. something unusual
   e. something that will be useful

6 When you meet someone for the first time do you:
   a. find it easy to form an opinion
   b. accept them readily
   c. reserve your judgement of them
   d. usually find them interesting
   e. try to find out more about them

7 When someone asks your advice with a problem they have, do you believe you can best help by:
   a. pointing out the immediate advantages and disadvantages
   b. rationalizing the whole problem
   c. focusing their attention on the values involved
   d. suggesting practical solutions
   e. offering a completely different approach

8 Do you believe you best solve personal problems by:
   a. taking time and identifying each part of the problem
   b. talking things over with other people
   c. adopting a speculative approach
   d. dealing with things one at a time
   e. going directly to the root of the problem

9   Which of the following do you consider is the most important in resolving a problem:
    a. exercising patience
    b. applying logic
    c. being flexible
    d. being realistic
    e. trying a new approach

10   Which of the following do you believe best describes you:
    a. challenging and enquiring
    b. receptive and supportive
    c. positive and assertive
    d. reserved and studious
    e. sociable and agreeable

11   Which of the following do you most admire:
    a. microcomputer designers
    b. writers
    c. surgeons
    d. statespeople
    e. businesspeople

12   Do you learn best by:
    a. doing something
    b. relating it to things you already know
    c. reading about it first
    d. experimenting
    e. breaking it down into easy steps

13   Do you believe the best way to influence people is through:
    a. logical explanation
    b. your enthusiasm
    c. being confident
    d. demonstrating empathy
    e. through debate

14   When reading fiction do you prefer stories:
    a. about relationships
    b. science fiction
    c. mystery and intrigue

    d. that are close to reality

    e. humorous

15 Having been asked to arrange a party, do you first:

    a. consider the budget

    b. plan one that is original

    c. ensure there is something in it for everyone to enjoy

    d. decide whether you need help

    e. decide on the most efficient way

16 A product which has gone wrong is just outside its guarantee. Would you:

    a. recognize that there's nothing you can do about it and let it go

    b. return it to the shop hoping they will replace or repair it

    c. see if it's something simple that you can mend yourself

    d. go out and buy a new one

    e. return it, point out the facts and see what reaction you get

17 When you go on holiday do you

    a. like to go with friends or family

    b. like to go somewhere new

    c. prefer to go alone and explore

    d. plan ahead to cover places of interest

    e. prefer an activity holiday

18 When planning to redecorate a room, would you prefer to:

    a. work out the best way using the advice of an expert

    b. use your own past experiences

    c. try something completely different

    d. focus on creating the right atmosphere

    e. do a small portion of the room to see what it looks like

19 In a business meeting do you work best with:

    a. straightforward positive people

    b. thoughtful methodical people

    c. those with original stimulating ideas

    d. those with practical and innovative ideas

    e. open-minded people with broad views

20   In a job situation where decisions have frequently to be
made would you choose to:
a. jointly make decisions by working with a team
b. have decisions made for you that enable you to get on
with the job
c. prefer to make the practical decisions and leave
theoretical ones to others
d. be involved before the decisions are made
e. be used as a trouble-shooter

See pages 11–13

THE IDEALIST

People who are idealistic want things to be good and right.
Consciously or unconsciously, they seek what they believe to be
the best possible for everyone.

They are easy to talk to; being open and unprejudiced they
welcome other people's ideas and contributions. They believe
that the world can be a better place and have a holistic approach.
However, they are often unrealistic (although with the best
intentions) and this leads to feelings of being let-down by others
and subsequent disappointment. When they fail to live up to
their own high ideals they can end up feeling very guilty or bad
about themselves.

They try to ensure that everyone is included, so that a family
outing will include something for Granny as well as the children,
and somewhere there will be a few hours for the husband to fish,
or for the wife to visit her favourite art gallery.

Idealists take a broad view of things. They like to have goals
which they will happily decide for themselves and others. They
need to be seen as helpful, open, trustworthy and useful but at
times they may appear too helpful which can irritate others.

They are much more interested in values than the facts;
working on intuition, they go with their gut-feeling. Because of

Question			P	I	R	A	S
1	a	I					
	b	A					
	c	P					
	d	S					
	e	R					
2	a	A					
	b	I					
	c	P					
	d	R					
	e	S					
3	a	P					
	b	S					
	c	R					
	d	I					
	e	A					
4	a	R					
	b	P					
	c	A					
	d	I					
	e	S					
5	a	R					
	b	I					
	c	P					
	d	S					
	e	A					

Subtotal A:

Question			P	I	R	A	S
6	a	I					
	b	P					
	c	A					
	d	R					
	e	S					
7	a	S					
	b	I					
	c	R					
	d	A					
	e	P					
8	a	A					
	b	R					
	c	S					
	d	I					
	e	P					
9	a	P					
	b	I					
	c	A					
	d	S					
	e	R					
10	a	A					
	b	P					
	c	R					
	d	I					
	e	S					

Subtotal B:

Question			P	I	R	A	S
11	a	P					
	b	I					
	c	A					
	d	S					
	e	R					
12	a	P					
	b	A					
	c	I					
	d	R					
	e	S					
13	a	A					
	b	I					
	c	S					
	d	P					
	e	R					
14	a	I					
	b	P					
	c	S					
	d	A					
	e	R					
15	a	A					
	b	R					
	c	S					
	d	I					
	e	P					

Subtotal C:

Question			P	I	R	A	S
16	a	I					
	b	A					
	c	R					
	d	P					
	e	S					
17	a	A					
	b	S					
	c	I					
	d	P					
	e	R					
18	a	P					
	b	I					
	c	A					
	d	R					
	e	S					
19	a	P					
	b	I					
	c	A					
	d	R					
	e	S					
20	a	P					
	b	I					
	c	A					
	d	R					
	e	S					

Subtotal D:

SUMMARY OF RESULTS

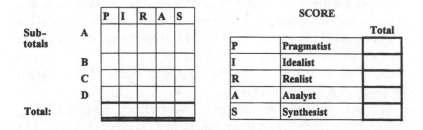

Sub-totals		P	I	R	A	S
	A					
	B					
	C					
	D					
Total:						

SCORE		Total
P	Pragmatist	
I	Idealist	
R	Realist	
A	Analyst	
S	Synthesist	

this they find it difficult relating to people with rigid thinking patterns or those based on logic.

They recognize where people think differently while believing that all differences can be resolved.

Idealists often fail to express their own opinions, going along with what others decide and then ending up feeling frustrated for not having spoken out.

If you live with an idealist you will be well cared for but you will need to recognize their high standards and need to be nurtured.

Example

Wilf works for a large superstore. He has been with this company for all of his working life. He is kind and considerate but often feels disappointed by people's responses and is frequently hurt by harsh comments and unfair treatment. He sincerely does his best for everyone, works hard and is conscientious, but recognizes he would be useless in a cut-throat environment, especially where money is put first. He is disappointed by the lack of appreciation shown to staff members by the management. In his own words: *They just don't care about people, they're only interested in the balance sheets at the end of the year.*

THE REALIST

Realists see life as it is. Only what they can feel, smell, touch, see, hear or personally experience exists. To them reality is empirical.

They may lack the ability or insight to see where perhaps there is another way of tackling a problem or accomplishing a certain task. However, the energy they put into doing things usually more than compensates for this.

They believe that agreement is essential in order to get things done. If you agree with them you're fine, if you don't it will be hard to get them to consider your point of view.

Realists are quick to voice their opinions and are sometimes a bit too outspoken for others. They have such strong ideas and beliefs about situations and things that they are often misunderstood and written-off by others as being pig-headed or inflexible. This is a pity as their way of looking at things helps us to keep our feet on the ground.

Realists function best when they are in control. They tend to over-simplify things in order to get quick results or co-operation, putting too much emphasis on facts as they see them. Wanting to get the job done can cause them at times to become impatient and intolerant of others.

Realists are straightforward; if you live with one you will know where you stand and can learn to cash in on their strengths.

Example

Jenny is a realist. She owns a small printing business which she believes can become very successful. She is intolerant of people who do not see things her way and of those who don't work as hard as she does. She tends to take on work without having done sufficient research – this prevents her at times from working with the confidence that enables her to feel secure. She just can't understand why people don't see things her way when it is factual and correct. She gets on well with her staff and they think highly of her. People who know her describe her as straightforward.

THE SYNTHESIST

The synthesist is a sceptic who not only finds conflict interesting but actually enjoys it. This often results in them being labelled insensitive and unpopular. Often they are seen as stirring up trouble when this is not their real intention.

They are always coming up with new ideas, looking for ways to make everything fit into a complex pattern, but in so doing fail to see that their approach frequently upsets people who do not appreciate their way of thinking. When challenged they may respond with sarcasm or irrational behaviour in order to protect their own feelings.

They find it hard to trust people or to believe that anyone is really telling the truth.

Synthesists like to drop ideas or suggestions into a situation to create something different or challenging. They love to come up with ideas that may seem inappropriate and sometimes infuriating. A friend who thinks this way suddenly surprised a group of us one day by suggesting that holidays were bad for people. After we had all strongly opposed this suggestion he then went on to justify his comment. I don't think for a moment that he seriously expected us all to stop taking holidays but enjoyed our response and the discourse.

Synthesists constantly use speculation: what if this or that happened? Or, suppose we tried doing it another way? They like to make things relate and/or to fit together in unusual ways. They love playing with new ideas and creating new combinations (useful if you're a scientist or inventor).

Sometimes they appear to be out of touch with the real world and one is led to believe that they do not take anything seriously. They push for change without pausing to consider the consequences.

Their original and challenging approach can be invaluable in business and their unusual sense of humour can lighten many a tense situation. But bear in mind that they are rarely cautious.

Living with synthesists isn't always easy but they do liven up your life and can give you a completely new way of looking at the most mundane.

Example

Joe is a synthesist. He creates a lot of aggravation in the family and with friends by appearing awkward and argumentative. He never seems to just accept anything and is always looking for other ways of doing things or people's hidden motives. He often appears to create an argument in order to watch other people's reactions. He spends a considerable amount of energy fighting for those he considers are getting a raw deal and writes frequent letters to Members of Parliament and newspapers. In reality he is very hard-working, conscientious, and sees unusual opportunities and ways of doing things that others miss. Because of the way he thinks he finds it hard to get along with people unless they see things his way – and even then he usually doubts that they really mean what they say.

THE PRAGMATIST

Pragmatists are essentially practical, down to earth people who like to get on with things. They enjoy taking new ideas and putting them into practice, looking for ways of doing things that utilize their experiences.

They do not understand procrastinators and tend to get impatient. *Why don't they just get on and do it?* is their response. All too often they ignore, or brush aside, long-term effects or theories, needing to see immediate results. In their desire to get things done they can become impatient and may appear far too accommodating or willing to compromise.

They love to bargain and negotiate and do well in sales where their natural thinking strategies come into their own. Take them along to a market for the day and you will make them happy.

They have little time for theories and whether something is true or false is determined by their personal experiences. They recognize that life is not easy to understand or to manage. Due to their own immediate (often unpredictable) response to situations they cause conflicts and misunderstandings with family and those with whom they work.

They thrive on praise and are at their best when they are in the limelight. They are good at putting themselves in other people's shoes.

The pragmatists' way of thinking is flexible; they are innovative, like to experiment, and are enthusiastic over new projects. Their inability to recognize or understand some people's need to plan and have structures around which to work means that they often fail to benefit from the strengths of others.

One of the advantages of living with pragmatists is that they are easy to influence: tell them there is no way the garage can be converted into a kitchen and they'll prove to you how it can be done.

Example

Jan is a pragmatist. She is a busy mother with two children and a part-time job in a store. She plans her day the night before to ensure things get done. She is practical and hard-working. Her husband says he's never quite sure which way she's going to jump next. She finds it hard to think about the children when she's at work, having mentally placed them in school and out of her way.

She is an active member of the Teacher and Parent's Group producing many useful ideas for fundraising. She is sociable and gets on well with people but tends to be impatient with those who take time to make decisions. She has no time for pro-crastinators.

THE ANALYST

Analysts use clear thinking approaches to solving problems and in the way they view life. They are stable and predictable, but expressing or understanding emotions often seems completely beyond them.

They are not very intuitive, approaching problems in a rational, logical, methodical way, paying careful attention to detail. They enjoy situations that challenge their thinking and like to find solutions to problems.

Analysts are interested in theory but rarely recognize this, seeing it as conflicting with their logical way of thinking.

Surprisingly, they often fail to pay attention to what they consider to be small unimportant issues.

Once they have decided on the best way of doing something they find it hard to change their perspective, convinced that it is based entirely on logical reasoning. They avoid anything that is subjective.

To feel secure they need to be able to accurately predict what will happen. They do not like to be proven wrong and take pride in their competence and reliability.

They make few close friends and miss out on the human side of things. They often appear difficult to talk to, appearing cool, studious, and remote. They readily judge things and people. Their inflexible attitude can cause conflict, particularly where their work is concerned.

Living with analysts means that things get done as they are reliable and efficient and make few mistakes.

Example

Jim is an accountant working within a partnership. His main interest outside of work is computers. He seems to have little need for close friends. He speaks comfortably only with those who ask his advice when he will go to great lengths to help them find satisfactory solutions. Jim tends to be dogmatic and generalizes about people, placing them in groups that satisfies the way he sees them. He is totally reliable and honest. Once he has found 'the best way' of doing something he usually refuses to – or is unable to – consider any other options. He will 'stonewall' in a situation rather than argue, convinced that he is right. Even when he listens to the other point of view it makes little difference because he has already made up his mind and will not move from his position. The fascinating thing is that he has no idea he does this.

Being able now to identify the way you think means that you can better understand yourself and how you approach life and problems. You will most likely discover that your thinking patterns are reasonably well balanced as I have generally discovered in my research. Having seen over 6,000 clients since I began in practice, and with many people I know really well completing my questionnaire, I found that most of us have two main thinking processes that are almost equal. My own way of thinking is almost fifty-fifty, shared between analytical and idealistic – though I do also use the pragmatist's approach at times and can, on occasions, be quite a realist. The synthesist's way of thinking was way down on my own scoring. This is not surprising as synthesizing turned out to be the least likely style of thinking, which is probably why these people suffer, finding few with whom they can establish rapport. This doesn't mean they are inferior but they do often have a hard time.

As you see, each thinking 'style' has its own advantages and disadvantages. By learning to recognize how you mentally approach conflicting situations you can use your strengths productively. By becoming aware of those areas where you find it difficult to think in more than one direction you can avoid many heartaches and misunderstandings. You will also discover that by recognizing the way in which others think you can exercise more tolerance and benefit from their strong points. When you learn to understand *how* people think, you will find that you are able to 'tune in' and communicate more productively.

HOW TO BENEFIT FROM USING THINKING STRATEGIES

1   First, learn to recognize your way of thinking using the questionnaire for confirmation. Remember this assessment is not concrete evidence as there will be certain situations where you do not conform due to your personal experiences or situation. The questionnaire should be used as a guide only.

2   Learn where your ways of thinking are most effective. Acknowledge your strengths and use them productively.

3   Be aware of your weaknesses; you can then avoid putting yourself in situations where you are least able to cope. You will also avoid creating too many problems, disappointment and misunderstandings.

4   Where possible, choose a working situation that enables you to use your thinking strategies to advantage. For example, if you are an intuitive idealist you probably would find it difficult working as an analytical accountant but would do extremely well in a caring environment.

5   Learn to recognize the thinking strategies of your partner and to appreciate his or her strengths. Develop understanding of his or her weaknesses – by doing so you can avoid pressurizing your partner in certain situations.

6   Acknowledge your achievements. This doesn't mean that you should become big-headed; realizing that without the gifts

freely bestowed upon you at birth you would not be able to see, hear, think, feel or use your hands or voice in the way you do, will prevent you ever becoming arrogant. So enjoy the output from your input.

7   Do enjoy your individuality, your uniqueness. You don't have to be like someone else to succeed or to be happy.

2   Know Yourself

Before we can hope to resolve conflict with others we first have to deal with our inner conflict that does, and will, affect all our behaviour and thought processes. Often, we are quite unaware of the triggers that cause a set response, or we fail to recognize that we have set ways of thinking. We do not see that we have choices and can change a behaviour that frequently causes distress, frustration or anger, not only in others but also within ourselves.

This chapter is designed to help the reader explore his inner self. It explains how to make productive changes without causing self-destruction; to understand the role one's personality plays in relationships; and how emotional involvement affects decisions and responses. Sometimes it is necessary only to become aware in order to take control. On many occasions we simply fail to see any other way than the one we have been using.

INNER CONFLICT

The greatest hurdle to overcome in dealing with inner conflict is internal dialogue, more recently known as self-talk. It goes on most of the time when we are not in direct conversation with someone else. That silent voice within can be making comments such as: *He must think I'm a complete idiot! I bet she's going to go straight from here to tell all her friends what I've said. I'll never be able to keep this up. Who the hell does he think he is?* Of course this self-talk may sometimes help you to feel smug, boost your confidence, comfort you or give you courage, but most of the time self-talk is hell-bent on making you feel worse than you already do. It can very successfully prevent you from doing something you know that you ought, or should be able to do. There is a lot of truth in the old saying that 'We end up believing that which we tell ourselves' – and yet we go on doing it! How can people hope to achieve anything if they are constantly telling themselves they will fail, or that it is all their fault, or that they don't deserve anything different or better?

To change requires effort, and very little is achieved in life without commitment. If you truly want to deal with inner conflict and negative thinking, it starts here. You make yourself a promise to become aware of those silent thoughts and destructive dialogue and to stop doing it.

Let's look at an example: Dorothy is going for a job interview. This is the kind of work she has longed to do and she would really like to get this job. However, she is stuck in a traffic queue about which she can do nothing and is anxiously checking her watch every half minute. *Self-talk steps in:* I'm going to be late. They probably won't see me if I don't get there on time. I'm beginning to feel nervous already. I wonder if they'll ask me questions I can't answer. I bet I louse it up and say all the wrong things. Oh God! I feel sick at the thought of sitting there, trapped in an office with half a dozen people all staring at me and asking me things I can't answer. I know I'll blush and I can't think straight when this happens. I don't know why I even applied for the job, I probably can't do it and anyway they are bound to have had dozens of applicants – it's really a waste of time me going, but if I don't they'll think I'm rude and I can't bear that. Perhaps I could phone in and tell them I'm ill.

Dorothy, however, is not late and in reality has plenty of time to go to the cloakroom, tidy her hair, calm down and present a smiling face at reception. But her self-talk has already destroyed her confidence. In the end she neither goes for the interview nor makes the phone call.

Note that in all this no one else was involved. Dorothy managed the whole thing on her own. She could have reasoned that sometimes, with the best will in the world, people are delayed and arrive late for appointments, and if those interviewing fail to make allowances for this, then she probably wouldn't want to work for them even if they did offer her the job. She could, if she had chosen, pictured them as being kind and responsive – really lovely people for whom she would enjoy working. Whatever attitude she chooses will not only shape her own behaviour, but also influence the responses she receives.

When you send out negative signals and people respond to them, it reinforces your negative beliefs about yourself, and because you are unaware of what you are doing, you believe their treatment of you only goes to prove that your negative beliefs about yourself are correct.

A tremendous amount of inner conflict is caused by a sense of poor self-esteem. From time to time it is essential to pause and evaluate yourself, acknowledging your strengths and weaknesses. The good thing about doing this is that you can then decide on a course of action that enables you to do something about those things you want to change or to improve. If your immediate response to reading this is, *I could never do that*, then this itself is a wonderful example of self-talk that you are going to need to change.

From the completely opposite side of the spectrum you may project your self-image as being over-confident, using a forceful personality to impress and/or intimidate. This behaviour is usually adopted in order to protect oneself. It may well have been the way you learned to survive as a child but really isn't the way to get the best out of life as an adult.

John was just such a man who had no idea that he created his own problems. Entering my consulting rooms he glowered at me from beneath a bulging furrowed brow. His wife had given him an ultimatum: he either got help or she was leaving him. He didn't believe that he had a problem, and even if he did, he was quite unable to see how consulting me was going to help. Within a few minutes he was dominating the conversation determined to force me to see his point of view and to agree with him that the problem lay with other people who were either stupid, super-sensitive, illogical, or operated by emotions instead of logic. He was coherent and persuasive in his own way, giving the impression that unless I agreed with him I was just the same as the rest of the morons he had to deal with. I let him talk for some time and then made a second appointment for the following week.

In the meantime I did a lot of thinking and decided that if I was going to help John I had to tell him the truth as I saw it.

'Do you know how I felt when you left me last week?' I asked him on his next visit.

He raised his eyebrows. What had that to do with him?

'I was exhausted,' I said. 'I'm sure you have no idea how threatening your behaviour is, or how, because you are good with words, you can so easily crush other people. My first feeling was that I really didn't want to see you again as a client. My second, that I should have the courage to tell you the truth. I have the feeling that few people actually communicate the truth to you.'

He looked at me in amazement. 'Do I really come over like that?' he asked.

I nodded. 'You certainly did to me.'

An expression of understanding flashed in his eyes. 'No wonder I can never keep my staff!' he exclaimed. (He owned a newsagents in the next town).

John went on to explain that before retiring from the services he had been a major in the army where the control of others had been essential. He then acknowledged that he had become so used to giving orders he had stopped seeing people as human beings. He was an intelligent and fair man. Giving me his first smile since we met he asked, 'Can you help me?'

I looked him straight in the eye and replied: 'I believe that between us we could make life a lot better all round for you, your wife and your staff.'

Returning to his naturally official role (it wasn't going to change overnight), he said, 'Come on, then. Let's get started.'

When he finally stopped coming I received a lovely letter from

John thanking me. *My wife* he wrote, *says to tell you that I'm not such a bad guy to live with after all!*

Whatever has happened to you in the past – rejection, embarrassing situations, intimidation, ridicule, punishment, failure, disaster – know that they belong to the past and you don't *have* to go on carrying around all that old garbage.

I received a phone call the other day from a lady who told me that she had come to see me in my capacity as a hypnotherapist ten years ago with a terrible problem of shyness. 'Now,' she told me, 'I'm so confident perhaps I ought to come back so that you can tell me not to be so pushy.' She laughed: 'Only joking. I actually love the new me and the freedom it's given me.' Yes, people can change, but first they have to really want to.

All too often the reality is that although we don't like the way we are at present, we are too afraid, or lack the drive to do anything to change. Sadly, we may also spend a lot of time building up imagined scenarios where we see ourselves as the victims and believe that we have the right to retaliate, to be angry, or hurt, or to act aggressively.

Now it's time to do a little honest self-assessment. No one needs to know about this, but it is something you need to do to enable you to make positive decisions and to move forward.

QUESTIONNAIRE

Someone arranges to come and see you but fails to turn up:

- Do you: a) Get angry and think how unreliable people are? b) Feel disappointed and that people are always letting you down? c) Phone to check if there is a reason?

Someone deliberately pushes in front of you:

- Do you: a) Think how rude they are and tell them? b) Believe people are always doing this to you? c) Shrug and decide it doesn't matter?

A colleague at work is offered the promotion you had expected to get:

- Do you: a) See this as totally unfair, march off and go and tell your boss how you feel? b) Believe the situation is hopeless and that you're never going to get anywhere? c) Decide to ask your boss to explain why you didn't get the promotion and/or perhaps decide to look for another job?

If you chose the first response in the above examples, you are likely to be assertive when upset but find that your response often results in conflict rather than resolving the situation. If you chose the second option you have a tendency to accept the role of victim which endorses your sense of poor self-esteem. If you chose the third you are quite well balanced, able to be assertive when you think it necessary and also to keep things in perspective.

However, avoiding conflict by *not* choosing the first option does not resolve the situation, neither does it make you feel better about yourself. The second threatens to turn you into a martyr without gaining anything. The third, where you make the decision to act by either investigating the situation, deciding it doesn't matter, or actively choosing to remove yourself, demonstrates that choices are being made which enable you to control your life without confrontation that could lead to argument.

It is having the initiative – and ability – to consider the situation and then make a decision that will give you the control you need. Also, it is very important to avoid the 'poor old me' attitude as this does encourage people to treat you badly. Even where no words have been exchanged, your body language may be failing to convey positive messages.

A silent message that earns respect and consideration would be saying something like this: *I respect me, I like who I am. I am a worthwhile human being and I am also prepared to respect you so long as your behaviour enables me to do so.* I have often had a lot of fun – and also learned a lot – by using this approach to cope with someone who is well known for being difficult, unapproachable and aggressive. To actually help in bringing out their 'better side' (often despite their initial attitude) can be very rewarding. My encounter with Michael is a good example of this.

I was, at the time, in charge of the department where his daughter worked. Unfortunately, she suffered from BO (bodily odours) and the other girls had come to me complaining that they couldn't work with her that summer unless someone told her to do something about the smell. This fell to me and so, using all the tact and empathy I could muster, I explained the situation. She must have gone straight home and expressed her distress which upset her father. The next morning he came storming into my office determined to make someone pay for the indignity his daughter had been made to suffer. I recognized him from my own youth and so, choosing to ignore his angry countenance, I welcomed him, showed him to a chair and arranged for coffee. I don't think anyone had ever shown him a more pleasant, charming welcome. This, in itself, caused him to calm down and to give me time to speak first. I asked him how he was, told him I had no idea that he was Sharon's father, and said how pleased I was to renew his acquaintance. All this had, to some extent, diffused his anger, but he was still determined to achieve his aim: someone had been saying things about Sharon that really upset her and he was going to wring their necks. I told him that I thought what he was referring to was actually my doing, that I had explained to Sharon how, as our bodies move to maturity and we begin to produce certain hormones, we also produce sweat that gives off an unpleasant odour. I said that I had dealt in a similar way with my own daughter when she had reached that stage in her development. I also went on to explain that until someone cares enough to point this out to you, then you are often unaware that it is happening. Well, suddenly he was seeing me as someone who cared about his daughter and not someone who had caused her to feel bad and to look conspicuous in front of others. He finally stood up, thanked me for what I had done and, saying how pleased he was that Sharon was working for me, he left the office.

I will admit that the anger he exuded was so powerful I had felt really scared, but showing this would have been an admission of guilt in his eyes and somehow I knew that. By treating him with courtesy – something I think he rarely experienced – and by freely admitting that I was responsible, I managed to diffuse the situation and keep control.

If you treat people as if you expect them to be reasonable and to return the courtesy you extend to them, you are far less likely to become involved in conflict. Sometimes it will be necessary to back down to avoid violence but it is never right to admit something is your fault or responsibility when, quite clearly, it is not. If you do this, you will end up with a poor opinion of yourself and an internal mental label of coward, manipulator, or liar. Always remember, if your intention is for good, no matter how wrong things go, or how they may be misinterpreted, you can still walk away with your head held high.

ATTITUDE

Sometimes we have an attitude that does encourage conflict and yet we are unaware of this. Teenagers in particular often present an attitude that almost screams at you to challenge their behaviour. Understanding why they take such a stance can help to avoid conflict. After all, they are struggling with a changing body, being treated like a child while believing they are adult, and still being told what to do when they need to make their own decisions. Their attitude is hard to live with sometimes yet understandable. We tell ourselves they will grow out of it or leave home, thus removing the pressure on the rest of the family. However, it is much harder to understand challenging, aggressive, or stonewalling behaviour in people who are supposed to have grown up and ought to behave like adults, especially, you tell yourself, if they are supposed to love you, or hold a responsible position in the workplace.

We may not like or condone certain attitudes, but understanding where they come from can help up to use the right approach – or response – and get the best results. If you are insecure you may often present an inflexible *I'm right and you're an idiot* attitude towards others. You have to be pretty sure of yourself before you can admit to mistakes or being wrong. Those who have been brought up to believe that *You mustn't let people walk all over you* feel vulnerable unless they play the authoritative roll.

You may be (or know) one of those people who argue about the most unimportant things without ever pausing and asking: *Does it really matter?* This, for example, may be something as simple as arguing over the name of a place, a past event, a certain date. Does it really matter whether Jim married in a church or a registry office? And what difference will it make whether you went with your Dad to a funeral ten years ago or not? Yet it is often this kind of argument that causes angry responses, or results in people not speaking to each other for days – sometimes even longer. Frequent conflict over little things usually indicates a much bigger hidden problem, so you may need to become a kind of observant detective to uncover the real cause. This applies not only to yourself but also when dealing with others.

Our attitudes are shaped from a variety of things: these will include our personality and personal experiences, the way we view things, our beliefs, cultural influences, and how long we are exposed to certain situations. If you have lived for a long time with a difficult man (this could have been your father) you may well come to believe that all men are difficult, demanding, selfish, insensitive, and the moment your partner, friend, or colleague does anything to remind you of this, your feelings are restimulated and you immediately rush to your defence – or to attack.

If your lack of confidence causes self-doubt, focus on the things you do well, on friendships where you are valued, on goals you have achieved, and on things you have accomplished. I once suggested this to a lady who was a mathematician and mother of two lovely sons. 'But I've never achieved anything!' was her response. She totally failed to recognize her ability and successes.

One way of dealing with difficult attitudes in others is to use a little compassion. If you can think how awful or unpleasant it must be to feel that way, you may be better able to tolerate a behaviour that, at present, they are unable to change. This isn't suggesting that you allow yourself to be constantly walked over, but it will help you to be assertive when you feel the need while tempering your words with understanding.

Attitude, behaviour, self-esteem, and the way we value others, all play an important part in creating or avoiding conflict. *We need to be aware.*

ANGER

When someone close to you becomes angry with you, it often diffuses the emotional build-up if you ask, 'Why are you so angry with me?' Or, 'Why is it so important?' Is this person upset because they think you don't believe them? Perhaps they are afraid to allow you to be right due to their lack of confidence. Of course these roles could be reversed and you may be the one experiencing anger. If this is the case, try asking yourself, 'Why is it so important to me?' Is your self-image being threatened?

Some people get very angry when they feel there is absolutely nothing they can do about a situation. They may have re-organized their day to collect someone from the airport at a certain time, and then the plane is delayed by three hours. The resulting feeling of impotence may escalate from exasperation to explosive behaviour. It isn't the fault of the representative or the airport staff, but frustration that cannot be appeased can have some people yelling abuse at the first person who gets in their way.

There are people who hold positions of responsibility at work who really must not make mistakes. These would include a surgeon where a life is at stake, or an accountant whose advice may save or break a business, a lawyer who may be responsible for someone going to prison or staying free. Often they carry the *I must be right* attitude into the home which can cause a lot of conflict over seemingly small or unimportant tissues. By looking for, and understanding the underlying reasons for this behaviour, you may find it easier to live with this kind of person. They dare not be wrong for their confidence would be threatened and the structure they have built around themselves in order to successfully accomplish their work is at risk. I'm not saying it is easy, but understanding does help and is better than angry confrontations.

Where you find that *you* carry home tensions and stress generated at work, recognize where your problem lies and remind yourself it's okay to be wrong outside of work some of the time.

When we are stressed or under pressure we become impatient. (Stress can also cause us to become physically ill.) People who find themselves feeling frequently short-tempered or impatient need to question what is going on. When you are almost constantly stressed you are likely to explode into angry outbursts at the slightest provocation. This behaviour acts as a safety valve that enables you to survive. A much better way is to use a relaxation exercise that will help to take your mind off your problems thus allowing you to wind down. This can be done before arriving home from work: while sitting on the train, or in the car before you start driving, even while you are walking. And, of course, it can be done relaxing in a comfortable armchair in your own home.

Exercise 1 – Reducing tension

1   Start by tensing your toes and then let them relax. Do the same systematically with your calf muscles, your thigh muscles, and then your abdominal muscles. Hunch up your shoulders and then let them relax. Make your hands into two fists, hold for a moment and then let go and relax.

2   Now take a few really deep breaths and as you breathe in and

out, notice the feelings in your body. Let go and relax. Finally allow a calm peaceful expression to spread across your face and let your jaw relax.

3   Picture yourself arriving home. You open the door, step inside your house or apartment and do something you enjoy: reading the newspaper, making a cup of tea, giving someone a hug, telling a bedtime story to a child.

Done that? Right, remember to practise this regularly, it will help to reduce stress and also to prevent it building up in the first place.

Of course, not all anger is destructive or wrong. In some situations anger motivates us to take positive action; this is most clearly seen when we become aware of suffering or injustices. If our feelings motivate us to try to help, then a great deal of energy can be directed into something worthwhile. But what we are considering here are situations where anger achieves nothing and leads only to conflict and the inability to resolve the problem. It is also important to bear in mind that anger can turn to rage and this may result in physical damage. There is never any justification for using physical violence on your partner (or anyone else) – if you get that frustrated or angry and feel yourself losing control, walk away and give yourself time to calm down. Being violent may subdue someone or force them into submission, but it does *not* resolve conflict. To believe this is to delude oneself; to accept such treatment is to encourage it.

A woman once arrived at my door with a black eye and admitted that it had been caused by her husband. 'But I deserved it,' she told me, really believing this. Two months later I heard that she had committed suicide. What could have happened in her life for her to believe she deserved to be physically abused?

When your anger does appear to you to be justified, see if you can tone it down to annoyance. This way you can express yourself clearly while keeping control of your emotions. Remember, the person who angers you controls you.

INJUSTICE

How do *you* deal with unfair accusations or treatment? Do you feel angry? Hurt? Disappointed? Rejected? Victimized? For most of us, when we are unfairly accused, we experience anger. After all, it's unfair! I recall my own children telling me that when they were punished for something they had done, they saw that as okay, but when they were accused and punished for something they really hadn't done, it hurt so much that they never forgot it.

Somehow it is even worse when you hear at second hand about someone who has unfairly accused you. The overriding feeling is that they should have known you would never have said or done such a thing.

There are occasions when we know that we are being unfairly accused or blamed and there isn't a thing we can do about it. If this is so, we have to let it go. Becoming bitter, letting things inwardly smoulder only serves to destroy us.

Often our problem is that we feel the powerful need to defend ourselves. We can't just let 'them' say (or do) such a thing and get away with it. Socially we feel a need to be heard, for people to know we are not 'like that'. We read daily in the tabloids of people who have accused others and the only thing involved is their reputation, but it matters so much that vast sums of money go into the lawyer's bank accounts and the courts, while these people fight on behalf of the accused. Of course it is sometimes important that a name is cleared, one's job or future may depend upon it.

Most people have a strong sense of justice and see injustice as being totally unacceptable. However, when it comes to conflict that ends up in the courts, or there is no possible way of proving yourself right without going bankrupt in the process, you do need to view the situation in a calm manner and ask yourself *just what am I losing*? If you absolutely know the truth in your heart you may need to question *why it is so important for the rest of the world to know*?

When Mark's marriage was on the rocks and his wife was

having an affair with someone else, he met Caroline. He explained the situation and some months later they started an intimate relationship. This was then used later by his wife as grounds and justification for her divorcing him. When he explained the situation to the solicitor, that his wife's accusations were unfair as he had only begun the new relationship after his marriage had become irretrievable, the solicitor's response was, 'Does it matter? If you want out, the cheapest speediest way to bring it to an end is to simply go along with the way your wife wants it.' Mark did. Knowing the truth within himself, he decided, was all that really mattered.

Examining your reactions and responses and learning how to deal with your own anger, aggression and the desire to retaliate or punish, can all be very challenging. The way in which you choose to conduct yourself can also improve the quality of your life and make the world feel a much better place in which to live.

We are not going to be able to go through life without encountering some internal and external conflict, but we do have a choice in how we handle it. Sometimes it can even be fun.

Useful tips

Learn to recognize your own reactions and then to question why you feel that way. Poor self-esteem means that other people's words or actions are often misinterpreted as insults or seen as trying to 'get at you'.

- Ask yourself when you get upset with someone whether it is the way they say or do something, or the act itself that upsets you.
- Question whether it is your attitude that is causing, or prolonging, conflict.
- Realize when there is no point in pursuing a matter and let it go.
- Don't be afraid to admit when you're wrong.

3   *Intimate Relationships*

Learning to live with someone is an ongoing experience. To assume we know someone so well that we no longer need to make an effort, or to believe that *real* talking is unnecessary, will lead inevitably to negative feelings. People's needs do change, and their needs and feelings have to be communicated if a close relationship is to be sustained. Living with someone doesn't necessarily mean you have a relationship – close communication does.

As we grow to feel safe within a relationship many fears and insecurities will diminish and often disappear completely, but where they exist they can put tremendous strain on a relationship. Failure to correctly communicate fears and doubts can lead to overwhelming misunderstandings. A husband (or partner) spending three nights a week doing rugby training can make his wife feel very much unloved or second-rate. Many relationships do flounder because the one partner, in trying to communicate hurt feelings, only succeeds in creating conflict. A woman who always seems to be entertaining friends or visiting her relatives can cause similar feelings of rejection with the man ending up believing he just isn't important in her life.

Learning how to express yourself, how to listen and how to find solutions or agree a compromise are essential to the growth and happiness of an intimate relationship. So let us learn how to avoid confrontation and misunderstandings, how to effectively express hurt feelings, how to recognize the danger signs, and how to deal with conflict.

The success of the most important relationship in your life will depend on how you value yourself and the other person. It will also depend upon how you express yourself and communicate your thoughts and feelings. It is not how you discipline the children, how you spend your time, how often you have sex, that jeopardizes the relationship, but *how the problem is discussed*.

If your husband seems to have spent the whole evening chatting to your best friend when you are out together at a party, accusing him of fancying her or neglecting you won't resolve anything. He might very well not have realized what he was doing or how it was affecting you. Explaining how hurt you feel and *agreeing together* a way that you can communicate this to him in front of others – perhaps by using a code word – will prevent a repeat of this in the future.

Clive, who actually adores his wife, is a natural flirt and had no idea she felt so hurt by his behaviour. Finally she decided to tell him. He confessed to me that after that he just stopped doing it. It wasn't worth risking their good relationship and so he learned to modify his behaviour.

No matter how poor your relationship may be right now, you can immediately begin to improve things. However, it will require effort, change, and an understanding of what is happening, and there must be a willingness on both sides.

Exercise 2 – Understanding your own responses

Recall a situation when something your partner said or did upset you . . . Now ask yourself the following.

1 Why did I feel upset?
2 Was I prejudging my partner's behaviour without giving him/her a chance to explain?
3 Was it really worth an argument?
4 Was I behaving in a reasonable, mature manner?
5 What did (or would) winning the argument achieve?

The flirt

6   How will my behaviour (or winning the argument) affect our relationship?

Pausing to ask yourself these kind of questions in the future will help to avoid many arguments that could have a long-term detrimental effect on your relationship.

Direct attack rarely gets the response you want, and indicating disgust or contempt towards a partner only further adds to the rift. Partners may become so overwhelmed by their feelings and their inability to make any headway that they resort to the primitive response of yelling and screaming. All this conveys is how upset they are – it doesn't solve anything.

Husbands, more than wives, survive in response to verbal attack by switching off. They actually stop thinking. This is a safety mechanism that happens when feelings are getting close to being out of control. If you don't think and don't speak, you can't get into an argument. The problem here is that this behaviour prohibits any kind of solution either. One has to work through problems not ignore them, refuse to discuss them or storm out of the house.

Sadie had been married for 35 years when she made the decision to start going out on her own and doing her own thing. Her husband, George, seemed only to want to come home in the evenings, eat dinner and then collapse in an armchair and watch TV. (A familiar story to many!) When the family was young, Sadie's life had been almost fully occupied with satisfying the children's needs, escorting them to and from various activities, etcetera. In the evenings, by the time they had gone to bed, she had also been content to relax in an armchair reading or watching TV. 'I want to do something with my life!' she tried to explain to George. 'We hardly ever go anywhere and I'll be old before I know it and I won't have done anything.' George didn't understand what had got into her. His response was to tell her to count her blessings, she should be grateful now to have a bit of peace. For himself, at the end of a day's work (he ran his own business which was very demanding both physically and mentally) he really felt that he needed to rest and the last thing he wanted was to have demands made on his free time. He may sound selfish, uncaring and insensitive, but he really didn't understand what Sadie was trying to communicate. Deciding at length that she had to do *something*, Sadie went ahead and started dancing lessons. Still George came home and sat watching TV, only now it didn't feel quite the same when Sadie wasn't there. He became aware of a feeling of unrest. Then one evening he arrived home to find his wife dressed in a new evening-gown just about to leave the house to go to a ball. He looked at her, noticing something that had been missing for some time: there was a sparkle about her, she looked excited, she was going to do something that made her feel good and he was missing out on all this. He gave her his usual brief kiss of greeting and headed for the stairs. 'Hang on,' he told her. 'I'm coming with you.' Then rushing ahead, he went to shower and change. After that he began to attend the classes and dances each week and they rediscovered something they had almost lost: the pleasure in doing things together.

Here is an example where verbal communication didn't work but action did. Remember, you always have a choice. Finding the best way requires mental effort followed by positive action. Nothing of value is ever achieved without effort. Sadly, a relationship sometimes reaches the stage where one, or both parties, feel the effort required to put things right isn't worth making; they either settle for indifference, which is terribly damaging to a person's self-esteem, or they spend years in unresolved conflict. In the end, a state of continuing disharmony may be all that is left of that once loving relationship.

Learning to become an active listener reduces stress and resentment. Fifty per cent of communication means really listening. When a husband announces: 'I think all those meetings you get involved in are a total waste of time', what he may be saying is, 'I miss you being away from me so much.' This is what I mean by *really listening*.

Much conflict between couples is caused because the sexes do think in such different ways. Often when the woman is feeling hurt, depressed or angry, what she needs is not the solution, but for the man to empathize. One woman, summing up this situation, said, 'I just want a hug sometimes, not ten different ways of how to put things right.' As she continued to speak I gathered that she cared for an elderly disabled mother who could, at times, be very difficult. The previous day she had discovered her mother trying to make her own bed and had then witnessed her collapsing on the bed exhausted. 'If only she would leave those things to me it would save an awful lot of aggravation and Mother having to spend days on her back,' she complained to her husband. He immediately pointed out that she could ask for help from Age Concern, or get in a nurse or home-help, or have her mother put into a nursing home. She already knew all this and didn't feel it was necessary; at that moment all she was asking for was a bit of understanding of her feelings of frustration – and a hug.

When men are upset they may need space to discharge their feelings by doing something active, or by relaxing at the local pub with friends – not necessarily talking about their problem but by removing themselves from any questioning at home. You have to get to know how your partner's needs are best met at these times.

Many men find a woman's approach to certain things so illogical that they tend to shrug their shoulders and opt out of the situation refusing to discuss it. This is a pity, for if real communication can take place, the practical approach he is able to offer, along with the ability to empathize, is invaluable.

Women do demonstrate more emotional distress than their male partners. When a woman becomes very upset this is an indicator of the intensity of her feelings, a way of releasing a build-up of energy. It does not mean that she no longer wants to live with her partner.

In saying this I am not suggesting that only men use logic, but research does strongly indicate that men's brains more frequently apply logic whereas women operate far more at an intuitive level.

EMOTIONAL BLACKMAIL

Emotional blackmail is a tool many resort to when direct communication fails, but it really doesn't work long-term. The other person may go along with this for a while but such behaviour is seen as degrading and insulting and breeds the desire to retaliate.

With adults, manipulation can be more subtle and less direct than the strategies used as a child, but they are nonetheless effective. Being sick, having a migraine, developing mysterious pains, are ways of manipulative control that can be surprisingly real to the sufferer but serve to disrupt the pattern of unacceptable behaviour and conflict.

A client told me recently how, when she cannot cope with her husband's moods, she actually starts to vomit and appears to have a stomach upset; this results in her spending a couple of days in bed. By doing this she has unconsciously found a way of initiating his concern for her well-being and thus an acceptable way of breaking the mood is established. He steadfastly believes that there must be something wrong with her and can see no connection between this and his own behaviour.

Sometimes people use manipulative behaviour without realizing what they are doing. But when emotional blackmail is recognized it creates strong resentment. We all fight against being manipulated either consciously or at an unconscious level. It doesn't feel good.

BETRAYAL

It is hard, when you love someone, to find that instead of them 'being on your side' they seem, at times, to enjoy putting you down or joining in the criticism. Just when you most need their support they join the opposition. This may occur when, for example, you have just finished planting out the garden and a visitor arrives. Your partner brings them out into the garden to see you. 'Shouldn't you dig over that patch first?' the visitor comments. 'And this really isn't the right time to move dahlias.' Of course all this is said without any thought of upsetting you. However, your partner then turns and says, 'That's what I thought. It's ridiculous tackling the garden this time of the year!'

How let-down you feel – it's almost like a betrayal. Whatever your partner thought, she could have supported you in front of a relative stranger.

Knowing someone very well, spending a great deal of your life with them, does mean that we often tend to take them for granted or make light of their feelings. In fact, their feelings should matter more to us than any other, but too often we brush them aside by using derogatory words such as: *Don't be ridiculous; You're so disorganized you'll never do it; It's no good asking you, you haven't a clue.* When this happens in front of other people it is even harder to take; defending oneself in public is embarrassing and painful for most of us.

We look to our partner to help build our self-esteem and feel let-down when they fail to offer support or criticize. Even constructive criticism can backfire if offered at an inappropriate moment. By treating our partners with as much courtesy as we would afford a stranger we are less likely to hurt or cause offence. Now isn't that a strange thought?

How do you cope when you are on the receiving end? How many times has your partner embarrassed you, ignored you or your opinion in company, suggested by word or act that you are of little consequence? Do you show that you are upset, do you silently seethe, or do you wait until you are home and then have it out with him? Maybe the moment isn't appropriate – after all, if you are at dinner with your husband's boss you hardly want to show him in a bad light. Nonetheless, you could ask him to spare you a few minutes, move away and quietly point out that his behaviour is hurting your feelings or offending you. If you're generous, you might suggest that perhaps he didn't realize what he was doing. If you wait until you are home the moment may have passed, it may even be forgotten or denied, or it may be suggested to you that you were over-reacting. If it hurts, then it is better to bring things out into the open and express those hurt feelings rather than harbour negative thoughts and destructive emotions. 'Sorry love. I didn't realize,' can put things right in a moment.

We are hurt most of all when our trust is betrayed. It is devastating when someone to whom you have committed your whole being, entrusted with your innermost thoughts and feelings, goes and reveals these to someone else. When a partner has an affair these kind of thoughts play an important role in how you cope. *I suppose he's telling her everything. They probably laugh together over me. I bet they are discussing how our sex life was.* In order to protect ourselves we turn to their faults, become very bitter, and the powerful desire to hurt back takes over. This may be physical: we read of those who kill their partners because their trust has been betrayed. *If I can't have her no one else will.* More often the hurt is demonstrated by using words to undermine the other partner; anything you can drag up is used and it becomes impossible in many cases to remember that you ever had a good relationship. All thought is directed at supporting your role of being the victim.

DEVALUED

One of the most destructive behaviours in a relationship is being made to feel devalued. We all need to feel appreciated.

Both sexes are sensitive to the way their partner views others; even when this is done from the armchair watching television. Men who praise the appearance of women who have good looks and fantastic figures are going to make any woman but the most secure feel inferior. This can effect one's freedom and sex life. The wife may come to feel so inferior that she undresses in the bathroom and is so conscious of her imperfect body that when she is touched it is difficult to enjoy the pleasures of physical contact and the sexual response is diminished. Of course something similar happens when women are always praising other men, although this might be pointing out their ability to provide materialistic things; few charismatic men on the screen are shown as being hard-up or a failure. Unfortunately, the recent open approach to sex, as shown on television, has done more harm than good, leaving many feeling inadequate.

A very good way of keeping a healthy relationship going is to avoid talking about your partner's behaviour to others, either in front of them or behind their backs. It's okay to express your pleasure or to share surprises, but to go on about how selfish, insensitive, or thoughtless someone is does no one any good. If you are hurt or upset by someone's behaviour the person with whom you should discuss this is the one concerned. If you absolutely can't – and some people will steadfastly refuse to discuss emotions because they don't know how to handle them –

Expectation plays an important role

then you may obtain constructive help by speaking with a counsellor who will be impartial and able to help you to get things into perspective. You can then make positive decisions as to how you might improve matters.

Words of appreciation go a long way and cost little effort. We need to know that we play an important role in our partner's life.

THE POWERFUL EFFECT OF STRESS

Stress is felt by people in different ways; what may seem only a little thing to one person can appear like the end of the world to another. In a close relationship we get to know those things that are stressful to our partner; this ought to lead to support and encouragement in helping them overcome their specific problem, but often we use scorn or ridicule which isn't any help at all.

People don't *choose* to feel stressed, and such comments as, 'Don't be silly, the decorators will only be here for a week!' when the wife is dreading it, isn't going to help the situation. Telling your husband, 'Forget work, it isn't your problem,' when the thought of tomorrow is keeping him awake, won't help alter the way he feels. Sometimes all you can do to help is to be present and encourage him to talk about what is bothering him. Enabling your partner to talk will help him to feel better. You may not have a clue what he is talking about but can still listen attentively as he tries to put his thoughts into words. You may even find that sometimes you are able to offer suggestions that can be implemented to improve the situation, or to help your partner see things from a different perspective.

When we are stressed we behave differently. This differs from one person to another, if your partner retreats into silence, this may be his way of dealing with stress – by prodding or nagging him to snap out of it you are not helping but only adding to the stress. Another person may drink to excess, talk incessantly, even have an affair – which may sound like an additional stress but which diverts the mind temporarily from the problem. Obviously, if someone retreats into silence for too long there is cause for concern. If they can't or won't talk, seek professional advice. One woman, recognizing how stressed her husband had become due to an excessive workload, asked how she could help. 'Just be happy,' he replied. This removed a further burden of feeling that he was letting her down.

A very good way to reduce stress and prevent depression is to do some kind of physical activity: join a gym or rambling club, start playing pool, or take up a sport. If this is not possible, any activity that involves both the brain and the body will help.

Fear creates stress which in turn produces a state of anxiety which can manifest itself as conflict. Knowing what is going on in your partner's life will help you to make the right moves. You will know when to stay quiet, when to encourage their talking, when to suggest taking a walk together.

Much conflict can be avoided by recognizing another person's character, understanding their thinking strategies, and accepting them without trying too much to change them. After all, this was the person you chose to spend your life with, so why try now to change that person?

How is it that a husband or wife can be perfectly charming and co-operative with everyone when he or she is at work but then come home and behave so differently? And when you try to enquire as to what has gone wrong you feel close to having your head bitten off! There are those who need to have a safety valve and use their partner without realizing that this is what they are doing. This can be seen as a compliment if you are able to recognize that your partner, who may have longed to explode all day at work but dared not, feels safe enough to discharge that negative energy at home. If you can understand this you may be able to make allowances. However, if it continues, the problem needs to be addressed. It is neither kind nor fair to 'take it out' on your partner or family.

Jack arrived home one day in a foul mood. His wife, Lyn, who had been home all day coping with three small children had put them to bed early, cooked a nice dinner, and was looking forward to spending the evening with her husband. But he barely spoke during the meal, found half a dozen things to criticize, and then stomped off into his study. Lyn followed. He raised his head and glared at her. 'Now what do you want?' he demanded. 'I wondered why you need to be so angry with me?' she said. At this he seemed to physically collapse, looked very contrite and said, 'I'm sorry, love. I've had one hell of a day at the office. It's nothing to do with you.' It was then so easy for her to approach him, put her arms around him and just hold him tight for a few moments. Of course she could have said, 'So have I! What makes you think you're the only one who has to deal with difficult people?' This is the kind of conflict we can so easily avoid if our intention is to resolve the matter and not to stand up for what we often mistakenly see as 'our rights'. *Communication not confrontation is the key.*

BEHAVING BADLY

There are some people with whom you cannot argue. This results in a feeling of helplessness and the conviction that they will always win, manage to reduce you in some way, and leave you feeling like a complete idiot. Often their attitude causes a complete mental blank which seems to endorse your belief that with this particular person you can't think straight. This is often why many women do not let their husbands teach them to drive; explaining with a sigh: 'He's got infinite patience with his staff but absolutely none with me!' This kind of thing can happen in reverse where the woman makes the man feel like a helpless moron in the kitchen so that he backs off and never does any domestic job.

The main reasons for such behaviour are:

a. it gives the person power which they desperately need to compensate for other areas in their life (they may feel very insignificant at work)
b. they do not value their partner's feelings
c. they need to feel superior.

There is another problem where caring becomes controlling; this is when it gives the carer power and/or a sense of identity and feeling of importance. Julie, who is a bright intelligent lady, married a man like this. He took such control over her life that when they went out for a meal he even chose the food she was to eat. After a couple of years she felt she couldn't tolerate his behaviour any longer and divorced him. Within twelve months she was dating another man with exactly the same tendencies. Here was someone who, in a strange way, needed that control because it made her feel special and important, and in a round-about way it enabled her to feel that she controlled him.

Treating your partner badly may be another form of back-handed compliment – you treat them as you would yourself. If you are in the habit of scolding yourself when you do something you consider stupid or negligent you may use similar words with your partner.

When we are away from others and in our own homes, we usually feel able to let down the façade that is almost always present to some degree when we are with other people. It's a bit like licking your fingers at dinner, you would never do it in front of strangers, but you feel you can with only your family present. This isn't meant as an insult to them but indicates that you feel safe enough to be yourself.

We need to be able to let go sometimes and home ought to be the safest environment in which to do so. If our actions are being misunderstood we need to explain them.

INDIFFERENCE

Indifference is very destructive within an intimate relationship. When the person, who is supposed to love you, seems to pay little or no attention to either what you are doing with your life or how you feel, it can be hard not to create an argument just to get attention. It's a bit like the child who sets his bedroom on fire – at last he gets noticed! Some people do let work or hobbies take over their lives without recognizing what is happening and fail to see how damaging it is to their relationship.

No marriage, or a relationship, is going to last unless we tend it with care. We should never assume things are all right and that our partner doesn't mind, or won't notice, or isn't interested. Using courtesy means enquiring of, and considering the other person's feelings.

'You don't mind if I go and watch the football, do you?' This is a question that defies you to object. Part of the question is suggesting that you are a good type who wouldn't want to spoil his pleasure. Another is assuming he knows you well, while the body language and tone of voice is telling you that this is something he really wants to do and he doesn't want you to deprive him of his pleasure. You may even find yourself making excuses for this man who has spent the last three nights glued to the TV set watching one match after another. After all, you reason to yourself, he works so hard and has little time to pursue his hobbies. Then there may be another little voice arguing, 'But he spends far more time watching football than he spends talking to me.' If something like this is happening to you, then you need to talk and to express your feelings. Keep the communication lines open. Stick to one subject when you want to resolve an issue, don't pull in half a dozen or refer to other things that happened in the past. You are far more likely to get a hearing if you stick to the issue.

If all this fails you may clothe yourself with apathy and eventually cease to care whether your partner wants to do things with you or to share your company. Woe betide apathy, it is the most insidious path to the destruction of a relationship.

Feeling unimportant in a relationship is another perceived view of a partner's indifference. If one partner spends too much time with the children or visiting her parents, the other may feel second-best and that he is of little importance. Once again, this may reflect poor self-esteem which results in angry accusations: 'You put everyone before me.' What is he trying to convey? That he feels neglected and worthless – and this hurts. These people need a lot of reassurance and demonstrations of love. It may be true that one partner is neglecting the relationship and even though the other may be well-balanced, even able to understand why, there is still a need to communicate one's own feelings.

AVOIDANCE

Often avoidance is used when people are not good at expressing themselves. If you're not present you don't have to deal with confrontations or emotions. But being somewhere else or with someone else, or being too busy to talk, usually only serves to drive a couple further and further apart. Going off to the pub or club each night, baby-sitting for a neighbour, or training for hours at the gym, may remove you from the scene but such actions do not resolve anything. Some people will even admit that the reason their marriage works is because they don't spend much time together. I would question what kind of a relationship they have.

People who can't cope with 'emotional stuff' often use avoidance tactics. When obviously in the wrong they may refuse to discuss their behaviour. Sometimes we just let it pass, but if it is something very serious, such as drinking too much, drug addiction, gambling, or spending money you can't afford, then something needs to be done. Trying to force them to look at what they are doing may result in denial or out and out conflict. Where communication has completely broken down and your partner's behaviour is destroying your relationship, seek outside help. You may choose to do this through your doctor, social worker, or go directly to the appropriate organization, such as Alcoholics Anonymous.

EMOTIONS

Emotions are really what conflict is all about. If we didn't feel angry, hurt, insulted, unfairly treated, etcetera, we would still disagree about certain things but we wouldn't get upset. One problem that we all have to learn to deal with in close relationships is the fact that, at times, we feel differently about the same thing. Someone else's experiences are going to be different from yours – at least some of the time – for we are all unique with our own history which determines how we perceive things and how we act or react.

In a close relationship it helps to focus on the positives. With this in mind you may like to consider the following points about your partner:

• What is there about your partner's appearance that pleases you?
• Recall a mannerism that you find endearing.

- Identify something your partner does that makes life easier or more comfortable for you.
- Name something he or she does freely for others.
- Recall the way he or she coped in a certain difficult situation.
- List three qualities in your partner that you admire.
- Think of a time when your partner was really supportive.

Now picture a situation where you see your partner relaxed and happy. How do you feel when you do this?

To improve your relationship, consider whether you perhaps need to change your attitude. When you know you are in the wrong ask yourself, Do I still search for justification or control? Or do I experience regret and does this cause feelings of guilt? Here is the moment to ask, How can I improve things?

Encourage your partner to talk about his or her emotions. Far more men than women try to avoid this: they are fearful of being put on the spot or being made to feel inadequate and believe it's better not to know. If you can approach this subject with an open mind, you will be amazed how enlightening it can be. You will know how to avoid saying or doing certain things that upset; you will have the opportunity to explain yourself and where your behaviour has been misunderstood; you will discover how to cash-in on the good feelings which can also lead to a far better sex life.

Learn to recognize when someone is at their most vulnerable. It is not constructive or kind to offer criticism or advice when someone is unable to respond positively. When discussing emotional matters it is important to find the right moment.

SEX – UNDERSTANDING WHAT IS HAPPENING

All too soon it seems the romance goes out of the window, the excitement has gone, and the unimaginative ritual that many couples sink into has them wondering, *where did it all go wrong?* Is it possible to still feel that flutter of excitement in your stomach when your partner touches you after a dozen or so years together? You may still love that person but are you still experiencing the magic? Do you stop and really *look* at your partner when he or she comes through the door after work? Do you plan special surprises for each other and evenings where you put the children to bed early and then give each other your total attention?

Much of the conflict and resentment that centres around how we have sex, how often or how good it is, has little to do with the act itself but with the ongoing relationship and the attention you give to each other. What most women regret is that the courting has disappeared. The man is disillusioned by the ordinariness of their life together. For both of them the spark has gone.

It is far better to deal with sexual conflict at an early stage in your relationship and the only way to resolve it is through communication. If your intention is to improve your sex life and not to verbally attack or accuse your partner, it is still possible, even after a number of years, to get your sex life back on track. If there is something you do not like or actively dislike, you don't have to go along with it; explain how you feel and search together for an alternative that can be mutually enjoyed. When your partner attempts to explain that there are things that he or she doesn't like, this doesn't mean that you are being rejected.

Each partner of the couple needs to feel loved, important, special, attractive, and here it's not enough to tell yourself you're still okay, as we grow older we need to see this reflected in 'the eye of the beholder'. Tell your partner how beautiful is the expression in her eyes, notice the shape of her ears, the way she holds her head, her smile – none of these things are going to change with age. Using words is essential. 'You will always be beautiful to me', can go a long way to making a woman feel and act desirable, but it needs to be sincere.

The way a woman responds to her partner will give him the confirmation he needs. Share with him how you feel when he does certain things; guide him so as to enable you both to enjoy sexual fulfilment.

Where the conflict concerns the number of times you have sex there is a real need to share your thoughts and feelings. When one partner doesn't feel like intercourse this doesn't mean they have stopped caring, there may be a dozen other reasons – worry often being one of them. If having good sex was an indication of our depth of love we would need to ask ourselves: why do so many people have one-night stands, brief encounters, or have sex with people they don't even know? There is a great difference between using someone to satisfy physical needs and sharing a sexual experience as an expression of loving feelings.

The major reason for conflict in sex, I am told by an experienced sex therapist, is that men and women are so very different. When there is an argument, for example, the man's way of 'making it up' and indicating that things are now all right is to make love, whereas a woman won't make love until the argument is over and she's feeling better about it. Tiredness is another area where we differ. A woman's response to sex is much more affected by tiredness than a man's. He seems much more able to put his sex into another box and often, despite tiredness, still feel the powerful sexual urge. Another area of conflict lies in the inability of the man to recognize that the woman needs far longer than the man to experience an orgasm – they also need to experience sex as part of the whole experience of being loved. It is not always vital that to enjoy good sex you must both experience an orgasm. When, perhaps for medical reasons, you are unable to have intercourse, you can still pleasure each other. Masturbation is not a dirty word, but an alternative that can enable continuing mutual sexual satisfaction when intercourse is not possible or advisable.

Here are some tips for a happy sex life:

- Turn complaints into requests.
- Be specific rather than general when you talk about your needs.
- Never use *should* and *always*.
- Never make an assumption – check it out.
- When you pick up on something being wrong, don't hide it, ask.

- Recognize the role children play in affecting your sex life.
- Communicate.

Where the man feels let down because his once, very sexually active partner, now seems to have lost interest, he may need to question what he is failing to do that used to be part of the enjoyment in their early days. Women also need to be attentive to their changed behaviour – especially after having children. The husband needs to feel that he still has a very special role and the wife should ensure that she encourages this and that she continues to make herself attractive for him. This demonstrates that he is important to her.

Our needs do change and sex can be enjoyed into our sixties and seventies, so long as we continue to communicate how we feel and how our needs can be met.

An unsatisfactory sex life is one reason why partners search for someone else. It is rare that one looks for someone else when everything is good at home.

When someone starts an affair the sense of rejection and betrayal on discovering this is so destructive that it is almost impossible to talk it through calmly. You feel hurt, angry, confused, perhaps even guilty. You may want to retaliate, accuse, yell abuse, punish your partner in some way for doing this to you.

There are a number of reasons why one seeks a second relationship or sexual experiences away from home. Because infidelity is such an emotionally charged situation, using a mediator may be necessary. Organizations such as Relate and Marriage Guidance have a very good record, and even if your partner won't accompany you, you can still be helped by talking through your feelings with a skilled counsellor.

People who are emotionally insecure often seek other relationships in an endeavour to prove something important to themselves. It is not enough that their partner finds them satisfactory, and with their problem they may move through many different relationships searching for a solution that can only be resolved by dealing with the poor self-esteem and often a damaged ego. If you have a partner like this, there is little you can do to put things right. You may take him or her back again and again, but unless the fundamental problem is dealt with, he or she is likely to keep searching for something that is never going to be found. For some men, sexual conquests prove their manhood, for women such conquests assure them that they are attractive.

IN THE WRONG

Admitting when we are wrong does not indicate weakness or that we are losing control, neither does it suggest submission. Certainly it takes courage to admit when we are at fault or have made a mistake, but doing so doesn't have to destroy your self-image or a relationship. Remember, it's okay to be wrong sometimes – you're only human. It also makes it easier to live with you when you are not *always* right.

When you are certain that it is your partner who is in the wrong, remember to ask yourself, *How important is it to correct him? What will it achieve?* If it is a little thing you may decide to let it go. If it matters, approach the subject calmly and if you feel yourself heading for an all-out row take yourself off and make a cup of tea. Give yourself time to calm down. It is difficult to see things clearly when you are very angry and this 'time out' strategy can be very helpful – so long as you don't use it to add fuel to the fire.

In an intimate relationship, most of the time, feeling loved is more important than being right.

THOUGHTLESS PEOPLE

You may find that you cannot change a thoughtless or forgetful person however much you try. Some people are just made that way. Often the thoughts in their heads are so interesting to them that they don't remember to leave petrol in the car, or to fetch in the washing before it rains. This doesn't mean they don't care, but that their priorities are different to your own. Such people are often very clever in a specific area and in order to pursue their thoughts they discard all those things they see as superfluous. The good news is that often they don't notice if the dinner is an hour late, or you forgot to iron a shirt for them, and will go out quite happily the next day in a creased one. They can be intolerant of people who waste their time if they have a strong compelling urge to study or complete some task. Scientists, physicists, artists and musicians frequently come into this group of people. Life can be tough on those who live with them but they really don't know that they often appear thoughtless or insular. They need people to love them and care for them who are not too demanding.

FREQUENT CAUSES OF CONFLICT

In my work I have noted certain areas that seem most frequently to cause conflict between couples. These are:

- different goals and values
- money
- interference by members of both or either of the families
- lack of communication
- boredom and lack of fulfilment
- putting careers first
- children
- hobbies and interests
- selfishness
- jealousy
- constant reminders of the partner's weaknesses
- alcohol and drugs

If only we had the wisdom to look at out goals before embarking on a long-term relationship we might avoid much conflict and breakdowns in marriage. However, when you are madly in love, you either ignore the fact that you have different goals or expectations in life, or believe they won't matter. When, later, different goals become important, there will be a need to sit down and discuss them *before* they become an issue. Sometimes compromise will be the only way forward. If one wants to go into politics while the other has dreams of living in an isolated cottage in the country, you may have to agree to someone else playing the supportive roll in politics – a secretary or friend perhaps – while the other accepts that they will spend many hours, even days alone. Suppose your spouse has always dreamed of going to live in New Zealand and you cannot bear to leave your homeland. One of you will have to be prepared to give up your dream or you seek a compromise, perhaps agreeing to try living abroad for six months of the year.

Money and how it is spent will always create conflict unless certain rules are agreed. Where one partner is quite hopeless at budgeting it may be necessary to agree to the other partner taking control in this area. When something is very important to you, try to analyse why this is so and then express your thoughts. What you see as important may simply be a status symbol which, at the same time, enables you to feel secure. In a case like this you may need to review your values and consider other ways of making you feel comfortable with who you are.

Annette, when she married Mark, insisted that he sold his old MG car in order that she could purchase bedding for the home. She thought this more important than an old car he didn't use, but to Mark his car had been the love of his life until he met Annette. They say love conquers all, but in a case like this she had been unable to appreciate his feelings and he had failed to convey exactly how important the car was to him. I often wonder if this was the beginning of the road to their divorce which followed some years later.

Interference by members of either family should not be tolerated. There is a strong difference between advice – which you may or may not choose to use – and interference. When one's parents have done much to help, it is hard to ask them to please step back and let you make your own mistakes and to run your life the way you decide with your partner. 'I love you Mum, but . . .' said without intention to hurt or reject is something most of us may have to use at some time. Then make sure that you arrange a little surprise, such as an outing in which they are included, to reassure them that you are not cutting them out of your life completely.

A number of stories filter through to me of couples, who once married, find themselves spending every Sunday at one or other of the parents' home. 'Just come for dinner,' you are told. Those parents are going to have to learn to fill the space you leave with new interests or activities. A friend told me how, after eight months of spending every Sunday with his wife's parents he exploded saying, 'I have a family too! But I don't want to spend every Sunday with them either. We have our own lives to live and I want to be home some weekends.'

Values too can cause constant friction if they are not understood. Have you ever tried living with a very tidy minded person when you are just the opposite? I've spoken with two couples who resolved this problem quite differently. In one case the tidy partner, to whom it really mattered, decided she would do the tidying up in areas where her husband thought it wasn't important. In the other case the husband told me that at first his wife's untidiness drove him to distraction, until he paused one day and asked himself which was more important, the tidiness or his wife? At this stage he made the conscious decision to lower his standards and enjoy living in the same house with the woman he loved.

When your partner is constantly reminding you of your weaknesses, faults or characteristic traits, it slowly erodes the relationship and damages morale. You probably already know what your faults are and don't much like them yourself. To be constantly told that you keep putting off doing things, or have a bad memory, usually only serves to make you feel even more inadequate. This kind of nagging may lead to you stubbornly refusing to attempt any change. When excessive focus is placed on your characteristic weaknesses and very little on your good qualities it can destroy your belief in yourself. You may feel the need to defend yourself, but having no defence you look for faults in the other person thus moving the focus away from yourself. It goes like this.

'You always procrastinate. Why do you keep putting off doing it? You know it's got to be done.'

'I don't *always* procrastinate.'

'You do unless its something you want to do for yourself.'

'You're a fine one to talk, by the time you got round to picking the beans they were so tough we couldn't eat them.'

'That was due to the bad weather we had, not me putting off doing it.'

'You always find an excuse.'

Nothing's changed, the negative feelings continue. You have allowed yourself to get on to the roundabout that can go on for hours.

If you are the one procrastinating you could agree: 'I know, I have always had this problem. I don't know what to do about it. I have tried.'

This could then be met with a positive response: 'Suppose we list priorities and put them on the memo board. We could tick them off when they are done and celebrate with a bottle of wine each time we complete the current list.'

Does this sound better? When you have to agree to disagree, having a code word can help. You first mutually agree to this and then, when either of you feels that the conversation is going nowhere and neither of you is prepared to relinquish your stand, you use a word or sentence that means, *let's call the whole thing off*. Remember, nagging does not get a positive response though it may sometimes get things done.

Boredom and a lack of fulfilment will often cause the one experiencing these feelings to attack the other. Quite often this occurs when the wife gives up work to have a family. Suddenly she feels so unimportant, has little to talk about outside her maternal role, and the future looks terribly bleak. When she tries to express how she feels her husband's response only adds to her misery: 'What do you expect me to do about it? You're the one who wanted to give up work and start a family.' True, but she didn't know then how living twenty-four hours a day with a small child can erode one's confidence in the outside world, and how unimportant other people can make you feel. Encouraging her to follow a hobby or interest outside the home will give her a sense of identity she desperately needs, and this will result in greater harmony within the home. And no, you can't change her life for her, but you can help her to feel better about the position she is in and also to ensure that she gets some freedom to follow other pursuits. If it is agreed that the husband fills the role of caring for the child and the wife returns to work after the confinement, the same feelings of insignificance can still occur. It is hard to reassure yourself that what you are doing is of immense value without any immediate feedback – in business our success is reflected back at us.

When one partner starts to spend more money on alcohol than is reasonable, you may try talking about it, but there is often strong denial that anything is wrong. You cannot help alcoholics until they recognize they have a problem. Pressure almost always creates a negative response. Arguments or tears will seem, to the alcoholic, justification for taking one more journey down to the pub, or opening one more bottle of wine. You may try expressing your feelings to a partner whose life is being controlled by alcohol, but if there is no definite sign of improvement it may be necessary to get outside support. Do not feel guilty about taking this action.

Drug problems can almost never be resolved by partners. Although you may think at first that there is no harm in taking drugs, the addiction usually escalates, also the amount of money involved means that – unless you are very rich – other areas of your life will have to suffer.

For several years Kathy lived with Keith, financially supporting his drug habit by working days in an office and several nights a week in a bar. She tried persuasion, argument, calm talking – gradually she sold everything she had to give him money he declared that he desperately needed. By then she was pregnant and giving up work made things even more stressful. Then, one day, she realized that nothing was going to change and that her first priority must be her baby. She gave up financing his habit, moved out and started a new life on her own. In a really negative relationship we need to know when to move out.

Selfishness is one more reason for escalating arguments and unless there is recognition and a change takes place, the partner may decide enough is enough. After years of argument, and if nothing changes, one finally gives up and leaves. If the selfish one has been allowed to always have his own way as a child, he may be quite oblivious to the fact that his behaviour is unreasonable. An intimate relationship is all about sharing and caring.

DEFENSIVE MECHANISMS

Everyone of us uses defensive behaviour at least some of the time. Let us not forget that as part of the animal kingdom we use defensive behaviour, when we feel threatened, as part of our overall survival mechanism. There are a number of different behaviour patterns we can adopt when we feel threatened: we may retreat into our shells, run for cover, stand and fight; or like the hedgehog who curls up into a ball when threatened, we defend ourselves by presenting a prickly exterior. In some cases we may feel perfectly able to cope with personal criticism but use an attacking posture if our families are threatened – albeit verbally. All these are natural defence mechanisms, the problems arise when we adopt one of these behaviours and the person whose words or behaviour is creating the threat fails to recognize what is happening. People who are normally easy-going, calm, agreeable, and willing to meet you more than halfway, can change dramatically when they feel threatened. There are many occasions when we fail to recognize that a partner has interpreted words or actions as threatening and are mystified by what we see as their unwarranted reaction.

In a close relationship, what often happens is that one partner unwittingly puts pressure on the other without realizing they are doing so. Their reaction may not be simply because they feel pressurized, but because they feel threatened.

With some people their defensive behaviour is always on the alert; it is as if they expect everyone always to be either criticizing them or putting them down. John was like this, and even when his wife, Hilary, made a comment that had nothing to do with him at all, he would turn it around and interpret it personally. They came to consult me when the stress in their relationship became intolerable. Hilary was threatening to leave. 'I love him,' she told me, 'but I can't bear the way he reacts to everything I say as if I were deliberately trying to hurt him or destroy his confidence. If I praise someone else's garden he will ask what's wrong with the one he made. If I suggest going for a walk he will ask, don't I think he gets enough exercise? When I tell him I've had a wonderful day out with an old friend he will say I must find life with him very boring.' John sat and listened in silence until I turned and asked him how he felt about what Hilary had just said. 'But she *does* keep going on at me. I can never do anything right,' he replied. 'I feel an utter failure.' He then added, 'She probably would be better off without me. I'll go if that's what she wants.' This wasn't what she wanted, but she didn't know how to communicate to him that when she spoke of other people it wasn't an indirect suggestion that he was lacking in that area. John was so stressed by internal conflict and a poor self-esteem that he couldn't allow his defences to relax for a moment. In therapy we discovered that this behaviour went back to his childhood and a very dictatorial father who always used every possible opportunity to make John feel inadequate or a failure. John's way of dealing with this was to try to be alert at all times and never to trust anything his father said at face value. Once John and Hilary came to recognize the root of their problem, they agreed on a code word that she could use that told him she wasn't trying to get at him or undermine him in any way.

Healthy relationships need time to evolve. Focusing on what

you mutually enjoy and those things you have in common is far more productive than giving unhealthy attention to your differences. Appreciate each others individuality and don't try to submerge it. I have known women who have hidden their skills in the mistaken belief that it would make the husband feel better. They believed that the husband would not be able to cope with a wife who was more learned in some areas, or had abilities or skills that he lacked. This does nothing to enhance a long-term relationship.

Imagine a husband who has been servicing the car for years, rushing home to change a tyre, and then discovering that his wife used to help her brother with his racing car and actually knows far more about mechanics than he does? Or the husband who never cooks thinking that this is where his wife needs to feel superior and she then finds out that he once worked as a chef? We also need to respect our partners.

FEELINGS DO COUNT

Some people maintain harmony by viewing their partner's idiosyncratic behaviour with amused tolerance. Once, visiting the family of my late husband's boss, I listened to him explaining some of the oddities of his wife's behaviour: 'Lisa can never go to sleep without going back downstairs and checking that the TV is unplugged,' he said. 'And she never cuts the meat until it's cold. When I practise on my guitar she always starts to sing.' But he viewed these habits with amusement, finding them endearing. He didn't allow them to annoy him and I learned a lot from that visit. Of course he could have become irritated or frustrated by her behaviour, but love helped him to find a better way so that their relationship was not damaged by criticism or nagging.

Have you ever planned a surprise that went hopelessly wrong? Do you remember how it felt? Did you accept responsibility or did you feel the other person had failed to live up to your expectations? It can happen with a secretly planned party or celebration of some kind; it may be a holiday, it could be something as simple as buying a piece of furniture for the home without consulting your partner. In Jane's case, it was to be a bit of decorating.

She had planned this for weeks. Normally they did the decorating together, but on this occasion she decided she would redecorate the hallway as a surprise. However, when Norman arrived home from work he walked straight through, failing to notice the changed decor. Feeling a bit disappointed, she pointed out to him the results of her labours. Norman looked and then slowly shook his head. 'It soaks up too much of the light,' he observed, 'And the colour doesn't match the curtains, though I suppose you could change those.' Now Jane was really upset. 'I've worked all day on this and you don't like it!' What started off as Norman simply failing to notice what she had done had moved on to criticism of her efforts which led to her mistaken interpretation that she was unappreciated. Conflict followed. It may have been an all-out row, she may have retired to the bedroom and left him to get his own supper, or she may have waited on him in stony silence with a marked diligence demonstrating how much *she* did for him.

When our expectations are not fulfilled we can believe that not only is the other person unfeeling, but that they do not value us. In reality they may simply be unobservant, tired out, preoccupied, or do not value things in the same way – what is important to you may simply not matter to them. If these feelings are not understood and negative ones are allowed to 'brew' the situation can become so distorted in the mind of the one with the expectations that she begins to feel nothing she does is of value. If this is a continuation of childhood experiences followed by the thought: *No one cares what I feel, no one appreciates what I do*, it can grow out of all proportion to the original act of omission. It can also prompt many rows.

Before getting into conflict that causes us to say things to each other that we may later come to regret, we need to consider the feelings of the other person. Some people are more sensitive than others.

JEALOUSY

It is like a monster that lurks beneath the bed, ready at any moment to show its head and take over your life. Jealousy can usually be traced back to childhood experiences and is very difficult to overcome. The most faithful constant partner imaginable can still, unwittingly, cause jealous responses.

Tracy came to see me because she was planning to go and live with her boyfriend but was aware that she was experiencing powerful feelings of distrust. 'It's ridiculous,' she confided, 'for in my calmer moments I know Paul is just not like that. He's never looked at another woman.' We did some regression together and she uncovered a painful experience from her childhood. She had arrived home one day to discover that her brother and two sisters had been taken on holiday by their father (who was separated from her mother) and she had been excluded. 'Mum tried to explain to me that Dad couldn't cope with any more children and that I would get a treat later. But it made no difference, I never totally trusted him again.' This was when the jealous feelings started; over the years they had grown to include total distrust for all men.

People struggling with feelings of jealousy do often misinterpret the actions of others. They need a lot of reassurance. Where they frequently suspect or accuse their partners of flirting, or having affairs, they end up destroying that which they most desperately need – a constant loving relationship. Sometimes their irrational behaviour will drive the partner to have an affair to justify the false accusations.

When you, or your partner, are feeling jealous, you need to communicate your fears and allow your partner to reassure you. I know it's hard, but try to keep things in perspective. Starting a row won't prevent you from feeling jealous. Where such powerful feelings are causing constant conflict, or undermining your relationship, it can be very helpful to consult a hypnotherapist who will help you identify the root cause of the problem and how to deal with it.

TERMINATION OF A RELATIONSHIP

There is probably more conflict and arguments when an intimate relationship comes to an end than in any other area of life. Although some relationships end amicably, and the two con-cerned even stay good friends, this is not what usually happens and there are intense feelings of pain, rejection, guilt, self-justification, fear for the future and, of course, anger.

Where children are concerned it is very important to try to conduct the termination with as little damage as possible to the family. Reassure the children – many children in these circum-stances believe that in some way the break-up must be their fault. Depending on age, it is better to tell the children – together if you can – that you have decided you cannot continue to life together and have decided to separate. Unless the children are really mature, they should not be put in the position of choosing which parent to go with. You have a responsibility and the children's well-being should always come first.

However hurt or angry you may feel, try to talk things through with your partner behind closed doors. These are your problems and not the children's.

Sometimes it is easier to talk things over in a place where you are more likely to keep your cool – a pub, dining together, or on a park bench. Whatever the reason for the break-up, getting angry, shouting accusations or using emotional blackmail is not going to help. What you want is the best possible outcome. 'I'll take him for all I can get!' is not a way forward if you want peace and harmony. You need to know that you have behaved fairly and can walk away feeling good about yourself.

A solicitor who is experienced in advising on divorce explained to me that a woman will often carry the guilt for the break-up, believing that in her role as homemaker she has failed and so accepts anything the husband dictates.

Fear for the future, or having too little money on which to exist, can cause unreasonable demands from both sides. If a man plans to start a new life and possibly a new family, having to pay over an unreasonable amount to his ex-wife can leave him feeling very bitter and resentful – it may also spoil any chance of getting things right a second time around.

Outside people can influence you to be unfair in your demands and solicitors aren't always the best people to turn to for advice as their job is to get the best deal possible for you. Family members are also going to be biased, so using an impartial person – preferably one you both agree on – could save a lot of pain and conflict.

Exercise 3 – Resolving conflict in an intimate relationship

Spend a few minutes reviewing a recent disagreement with your partner that did not have a satisfactory outcome . . .
Now answer the following questions:

- What were you thinking?
- What did you feel?
- Did you experience the need to defend yourself? If so, what defensive behaviour did you use? Angry verbal attack? Silence? Refusal to listen?
- Did you turn the situation around and blame him or her?
- Were you able to look at the issue objectively?
- Did you stick to the cause of the conflict or drag in other times or examples to support your position?
- Did you feel hurt, unfairly victimized?
- Did you find you were always being made to feel that you were the one in the wrong?

Close your eyes and picture the scene again only this time: Avoid blaming anyone; don't drag in old conflicts or behaviours; stick to the issue; see how you could have resolved the conflict by using a more positive approach and really considering the other person's views. Create a satisfactory outcome. Finally, make yourself a promise to use this approach next time you get into an argument or conflict.

To build on your relationship:

- Value it
- Learn to be content with the one who shares your life – searching mentally for someone better or different rarely works, the grass on the other side of the fence isn't any greener, it's only your perception of it
- Avoid comparisons
- Exercise tolerance – most people don't set out to cause aggravation, to upset or hurt, but we are all human with all the frailties that go with being human
- Use forgiveness – it offers wonderful healing

4 Family Conflicts

We all get involved in rows occasionally, and most families experience conflict from time to time. Some conflict is actually good for us when it occurs in a safe environment. Within the security of home we can learn to practise our responses, develop strategies that work, and learn how to handle our emotions. Hopefully, we also learn how to use anger productively and to develop other survival responses such as fear and caution.

In the security of home we learn to practise our responses

By the time we are out in the world we will have learned many skills that enable us to cope in a positive manner with our colleagues at work, neighbours, friends, brief encounters with strangers and, of course, intimate relationships.

Unfortunately, many people never get beyond their own front door when it comes to learning techniques to resolve conflicts. Insults, sarcasm, threats, physical violence are all used because those involved have never found a better way of saying or doing things. We believe that those closest to us *ought* to know better, that they *should* know what hurts, and that they *could* treat us differently if they chose to do so. The truth is that those closest to us often do not have the ability to step back and see us as separate people with feelings that are real and that matter to us. Harsh words uttered in moments of anger can have long lasting effects. When they are uttered by those whom we believe love us, or at least should understand us, the hurt can leave open wounds that fester until it seems nothing can ever heal them.

The good news is that understanding and appreciating other members of the family can be learned and implemented at any time. Sibling rivalry, when understood, does not have to destroy a family. Certainly learning the right skills in communication can bring a deeper understanding, you can learn and earn respect from those closest to you. However, we do need to know how to handle envy, jealousy, greed, criticism, guilt, and how to turn around negative reactions and build positive constructive behaviours. We also need to learn how to control our tempers.

FAIR TREATMENT

With this book in mind I asked my neighbours, who are in their seventies, if they had ever had any serious conflict within their family. They shook their heads.

'What is the secret?' I asked.

'Don't let things escalate,' she replied. 'As soon as anything bothers you, talk it over.'

This is a second marriage for each of them as they were both widowed and they have several children from their first marriages.

'We treat them all the same,' her husband told me. 'You wouldn't know which child or grandchildren belonged to either of us.'

Treating all the family with fairness is sometimes hard to do when the needs of one member are far greater than the others. If one child is homeless and another has his own house and obviously doesn't need help, it may be very difficult to hold back because you can't afford to give equally to both. You may have to ask yourself the question, 'Do we give equally, irrespective of their needs, or do we do what we feel is best at the time?' Some may say that as adults your children have to fight their own battles and resolve their own problems. You will have to make your own decisions according to your ethics and values. It does help to explain why you have made a certain decision that is likely to cause conflict if not understood. Again and again we come back to communication, it can prevent or resolve so many conflicts.

MANIPULATION

We all use manipulative behaviour as children. You just know that your mother can't put up with a tantrum in certain situations, so it is a wonderful moment to get your own way.

By the time we have matured we ought to have found better ways of getting co-operation, but when this fails we tend to fall back into the childish mode that used to work – at least some of the time.

If someone suggests that you are being manipulative, before rushing to defend yourself, carefully examine the evidence. We do sometimes use this type of behaviour without realizing it. Using words or actions that suggest someone close to you is selfish, guilty, inadequate or unattractive can all help in the manipulative game. By making people feel bad about themselves you can usually get them to come round to doing things the way you want. Manipulation should not be used if you wish to prevent bad feelings or open conflict.

Elderly people quite often use manipulative behaviour and because it is not easy to point this out to them, other family members can find themselves manoeuvred into doing all kinds of things they would rather not do because they don't know how to refuse.

DEVELOPING STRATEGIES

Some behaviour and responses are in-built, others we learn to copy; we also have our individual personalities that affect the way we view situations. We really do need to learn to recognize which strategies we are using and under what circumstances. To respond with anger where it enables you to stay alive is a good thing; to use threatening body language in a jostling queue is not. Adopting a quiet distant stance at a family gathering is okay if that's part of the way you gradually merge. Going straight in and chatting to someone who happens to look a little lonely is okay too. However, if you are using a certain kind of behaviour because you feel threatened, or have problems with your own identity, or because of the way in which you are viewing others, then life can feel a lot better if you find out 'why' you behave in that way. Having been hurt in the past you may back off to avoid experiencing those feelings again, but this doesn't resolve anything and can lead to an impoverished emotional life. When you understand the 'why' you can begin to do something to change such debilitating behaviour.

If you need help in this area you may benefit by reading my book *Are You In Control?* (*see* Further Reading).

There are times when we may suppress certain emotions, choosing to deal with them in our own way or leaving them until a later time when we feel more able to discuss them. Suppression is different from repression, it is a deliberate choice to inwardly control certain feelings and, although this may cause some immediate discomfort it can, at times, be the wisest course.

Here are some questions to ask yourself that will help in a situation that is creating conflict within the family:

- Why does it matter to me?
- Why do I react instead of respond?
- Why do I feel badly treated?
- Why do I feel misunderstood?
- If I win what does it achieve?

Tips that will help in an argument:

- Try to remain calm.
- Recognize when points of view are simply different and not necessarily wrong.
- When you pass judgement focus on the issue not the person.
- Recognize when defensive behaviour is being adopted and learn how to change it to positive communication.
- Stop using blame.
- Admit when you are wrong.
- Learn when to step back and take time away from the situation (do something else for a while – cool down).
- Where you prove your point, try to help the other person so that the argument does not destroy their self-esteem or your relationship.
- Resolve long-term conflict/disagreement so that it does not get resurrected in the future.

Linda had a very poor relationship with her father, and although she had two children she rarely took them to see him despite his constant phone calls and letters.

'I just can't forgive him for the way he treated Mum,' she told me. 'I know he's lonely but that's his own fault. He should have thought of that years ago. He left everything to Mum. She was an absolute slave to him.'

I told her that I thought he was probably sorry and regretted some of his past behaviour. I also suggested that perhaps the children would benefit from seeing their grandfather.

'That's his loss!' she exclaimed. 'He doesn't deserve kindness.'

Behind her words were feelings that ran very deep. She was angry, sad, bitter and also felt guilt. Each time we met the conversation would somehow come round to her father.

'What would you like to be able to do about it?' I asked.

'I'd like to tell him exactly how I feel,' she responded.

'Would that make you feel better?' I enquired.

She was silent for a few minutes and then turned to me and speaking softly said, 'I suppose it wouldn't improve the situation, would it?'

'It depends how you do it,' I ventured. I went on to explain that if her intentions were good and that she really wanted to communicate how and why she felt so reluctant to take the children to see him, perhaps they could work things out together.

'But it won't do any good if you spend the time just telling him how rotten he has been,' I said.

I didn't see her for some weeks after that and then one day she phoned. 'Guess what?' she began. 'I went to see Dad. I told him how miserable and sad I felt and how I'd even found myself wishing he had died instead of Mum. He broke down and cried and told me he felt the same. He said he couldn't undo the past and he didn't feel there was any point in going on living. I never thought in a million years that he would ever cry over anything. I had no idea he felt like that.'

All the anger and negative feelings had dissolved. Forgiving him, she discovered, had, in the end, been so easy.

'We're planning to go on holiday together and take the children. Can you imagine that? I guess he'll still drive me crazy occasionally – but do you know what? I actually love that awkward, bossy, stubborn man.'

NAGGING

There are few things within the family structure that cause more conflict than disregard for the value of others and being accused of nagging. Let us look at the structure of a typical example. As you will see this can be done in a variety of ways.

Crime: Leaving the bathroom light on.

Parent to child	Child to parent
1 *Accusation.* You always leave the light on!	*Denial.* I don't *always* leave it on!
2 *Sarcastic.* You paying the electricity bill, then?	*Attack.* Don't you ever think of anything except money?
3 *Derogatory.* You're hopeless! You can't even remember to switch off the light.	*Retaliation.* I suppose you never forget anything?
4 *Request.* Could you please try to remember to switch off the light?	*Response.* Okay. Sorry.

The 'request' used opens up an opportunity to communicate and to perhaps even find a solution to the problem. But suppose that no matter what you say you still get a negative response? You may then have to accept the situation, put in a smaller light bulb, or decide it really isn't important. Continued nagging may eventually get the desired result but won't promote good feelings and the next time you make a similar observation the old nagging may be resurrected giving ammunition to the guilty one.

A neighbour told me that her husband always wakes her up when he gets out of bed in the night and if she dozes off after lunch he deliberately wakes her. 'Well, she doesn't want to spend her life sleeping,' he said. It sounded unreasonable to me for they are both retired, but her words made me re-think the situation: 'Oh, he'll never change,' she said. 'He can't abide the thought that we're wasting our lives sleeping.' The smile she then bestowed on him showed that her love for him dealt with the issue far more effectively than arguing or nagging.

Annie, describing to me the rift with her mother-in-law, told how she was always nagging, disapproving of the way they spent their money and pointing out that they never saved. 'What right has she to criticize? It's not her money or her life.' I knew the lady in question and was surprised to hear these comments. A few days later I happened to meet her, and without any prompting from me she explained how worried she was about her family. 'Annie is a lovely girl,' she said, 'and I know she would like to return to her career, but she needs two years to complete her training which came to a halt when she had the baby and they just don't know how to save. I try to offer constructive advice but this only seems to make her angry and resentful.' It's useful to remind oneself occasionally that things are not always as they seem, or as we interpret them.

THE PROBLEM WITH CHILDREN ...

The way we see our parents behave towards each other will have a powerful effect on the way we in turn behave. We learn to be tolerant, violent, to demonstrate anger, to love, care for others, show compassion and so on in much the same way our parents did. Later we will come to be influenced by other family members, friends and school. By then much of the groundwork will have been done and, as our parents seem godlike to us when we are young, we believe that their example is the one to follow. If there is already a lot of conflict or suppression in the home we may rebel and take the opposite road, but you will have witnessed for yourself how often children grow up to be like their parents.

If you are not happy with your own feelings or responses this may be the moment when you need to reflect on the influences from your childhood. Try to recognize if you are using behaviours that evolved from them rather than ones you have consciously chosen as an adult.

People who readily resort to anger are often holding on to childhood behaviour. As children, getting angry may have been the only way to be heard, or noticed, or to get them what they wanted. Weak parents may have submitted to this kind of dominant behaviour, failing to stand firm or to discipline and follow through rules that would have taught the child his behaviour was unacceptable.

Violent and disruptive behaviour of children at home and in schools causes terrible distress and disorder. These children seem to lack the ability to pause and consider the effects of their behaviour. We are currently hearing of schools that are totally losing control because of the violent behaviour of even small children who have never learned to respond to discipline. It has been found that where this behaviour persists, involving the children in physical activities and competitive sport does help. These enable the build up of energy to be released safely. Sometimes the problem is due to a chemical disorder of the brain which needs professional diagnosis and treatment – although with very small children medication is not recommended.

Most mainstream schools lack the resources to supply specialist teaching and supervision and so have no choice but to suspend or expel pupils who cause disruption in the class. The teacher's priority is to protect other pupils and staff. Having a stand-up row with a teacher will not help your child, but your co-operation with school staff will.

Compulsory National Service was, arguably, a very helpful training ground in teaching young men control and how to fit into society – they had to learn to live and work with others. Since this ended, we have seen a rise in uncontrollable anger and destructive disruptive behaviour.

Unless parents agree certain rules and endeavour always to support each other in front of the children, they are going to encounter problems. People who have never had the job of bringing up children before, can have surprisingly strong views about what they should and shouldn't be allowed to do. Where parental beliefs conflict, the children quickly learn to play one parent off against the other. Perhaps without realizing it, one parent will undermine the other so that control becomes impossible. Consistency is so important when dealing with children – they need to know where they stand and stated boundaries enable them to feel safe. Constantly changing the rules will eventually lead to a confused child who finds it hard to operate in the outside world. Talking things through, agreeing rules and supporting each other, however hard this may seem at times, will strengthen the parent's position. However, it is worth remembering that rules should not be set in concrete and sometimes it will be necessary to negotiate.

There is going to be some conflict with your children as you endeavour to bring them up to be caring, responsible adults. This is natural and forms part of the training ground that will hopefully enable them to live in harmony with others later. Children will always be pushing against the boundaries you decide, and, from time to time you will need to review these boundaries. Rules and conditions enable you both to feel safe and if they can be made jointly there should be less conflict. More help on resolving conflict with teenagers is given in my book *13–19* (*see* Further Reading).

INTENTIONS

When you feel yourself sliding into an argument, try asking yourself why. What is your aim? Do you want to hurt? Hit back? Teach a lesson? Punish? Or do you want a satisfactory outcome? When you know that you are in the wrong (and that's not always clear in the heat of the moment) it does no harm to apologize, explain what you had been feeling at the time, ask the person to forgive you. You may, on the other hand, search for justification that's going to make you feel better – this isn't however, going to improve the relationship. A reasonable person is usually more than willing to accept an apology. It is good to remind ourselves occasionally that the person's intention may have been quite different to the way (or ways) in which we interpreted their words or deed.

Let's look at a few of these.

a. You offer to help someone and they refuse. Maybe they are not rejecting you but trying to remain independent or save you the trouble.
b. You tell someone something in confidence and then discover they have repeated it to someone else. Perhaps they forgot they were not supposed to speak of it, or they may have allowed the excitement of the revelation to carry them too far and it wasn't until afterwards they remembered that it had been confidential e.g. a son landing a new job, a daughter-in-law expecting a new baby.
c. You did something that, in your eyes, made you look really silly and your parent, who witnessed it, told everyone. They may really have found it funny and to share the story wasn't meant to degrade you or make you look stupid.

Ah well! These things are going to happen from time to time. The way to avoid conflict is to know your intentions and to feel good about who you are.

LONG-TERM CONFLICT

Flashes of anger are rarely taken too seriously and are usually soon forgotten, but conflict that is sustained over a long period needs to be addressed. Long-term conflict within families is a cause for concern and is likely to result in lasting damage to the family structure if not resolved. All too often we hear of families who haven't spoken for years, some taking family members to the courts over issues that ought to be sorted out by sitting round the table together and talking it through.

Often the cause of such conflict is prompted by jealousy, greed, fear or misunderstanding. Jealousy is a very painful emotion and colours every area in a relationship – it not only destroys harmony but will also destroy the person who is unable to come to terms with the emotion. If a brother and sister have grown up with feelings of jealousy, they will tend to perceive every situation with resentment and will be incapable of being impartial in their judgements.

Sarah has recently been promoted at work and her mother is passing on the good news to her brother, Peter.

'I wonder who she had to suck up to in order to get that,' he responds.

Mother, quite shocked replies: 'Sarah isn't like that! She is very conscientious and good at her job.'

Peter shrugs, 'They must be short on staff. I wouldn't put her in a position of authority.'

'Why ever not?'

'Oh, mother!' Peter sighs. 'You know Sarah. She'll try to be fairy godmother to everybody and that doesn't work when you're in charge. You have to be able to control people and Sarah doesn't, she manipulates them.'

By this time the mother is upset, wishing her two children liked each other, wondering where she went wrong, helpless to change anything. She could argue Sarah's case but realizes this will only alienate Peter further, for part of his problem is that he needs all his mother's praise and approval for himself.

'You never could see anything wrong in her!' he explodes angrily (though in reality he isn't really angry but by now is feeling very hurt).

'I see faults in both of you,' she protests, 'but I also see all the wonderful things you have both achieved and I'm very proud of you.'

Slightly mollified he kisses her cheek and turns to leave the house. Outside he meets his brother, Jack.

'Hey!' Jack greets him. 'Heard the good news? I've just landed that big contract I was telling you about.'

'Great! I hope it goes well, you deserve a break,' Peter says.

What is the difference? He feels no threat from his brother, there was never any competition between them and their parents treated them alike. But Sarah had been different, she was a girl, and he had been aware that in many subtle ways his parents were softer on her. When she cried his dad would always put her on his lap and comfort her, but when *he* got upset no one took any notice. Remember, this is the way *he* recalls things from his view point. He climbs into his car wondering why he feels so bad about Sarah. Other people like her and, he admits, if she was in real trouble he'd do anything to help her. The best thing, he decides, is to avoid seeing her and any time his mother turns the conversation towards her he'll just keep quiet. This is using avoiding tactics which will prevent any outward conflict, but they are not going to resolve his inner conflict or make him feel better towards his sister.

How could this situation be resolved? First Peter has to recognize that he has a real problem caused, not by his sister's behaviour, but by the way he feels. Then he needs to spend time with his sister and talk through the problem. If they care for each other – and in this case we know they do – then she will help him to overcome the gnawing jealousy that is destroying any hope of peace. Perhaps she might have a word with her parents suggesting that they make an effort to demonstrate their feeling for him. Many times parents fail to recognize that their son's feelings, often discounted in our society where men are supposed to be 'tough and not cry', are as real as a daughter's. There will still be occasions when Peter experiences the old jealous feeling raise its head, but having become aware, he should be able to recognize when this is happening. By using a little positive self-talk he will be able to prevent his feelings from escalating out of control.

When you are being criticized and you know that you *are* in the wrong, try using the following procedure:

Someone says to you, 'You always dominate the conversation when I bring my friends home.'

1   Admit it. (You should feel safe enough to do this within the family.)
2   Indicate when you recognize the criticism is fair. *I didn't realize I did that.*

3 Voice future intention that will avoid further conflict. *I'll try to remember and take a back seat next time.*

When you are certain that you are right and just in *your* criticism of a member of the family it is wise to:

1 State your case. *You are not pulling your weight around the house.*
2 Listen to their response and try to understand – empathize. *I'm so tired when I get home from work (or school).*
3 Exercise patience, understanding, tolerance. *I understand, but perhaps you need to organize your time so that you don't waste it.*
4 Be assertive and stand your ground if appropriate. *I'm going to set you some tasks that you can fit into the weekends and I expect them to be done.*

ACTIONS DON'T ALWAYS SPEAK LOUDER THAN WORDS

I am surprised how many young adults feel their parents don't really care about them because they never say so. 'But I'm always there for you' or 'Didn't I buy you your car?' or 'You should know I'd do anything for you', are the kind of responses they get when they question the parent. Many people do believe that actions speak louder than words and there isn't any need to keep telling people how you feel. If it happens too frequently there may be a ring of insincerity about it, sounding as if it is being said more from habit than from a spontaneous emotion. The truth is that most of us need to be told occasionally.

There are many people who really care very much about each other but find it impossible to put their feelings into words; this is often because they never heard or witnessed love being demonstrated when they were young. With some folk such demonstrations of feelings or words are embarrassing. I recall seeing an old friend last year whom I hadn't spoken to for some time and discovered he had been quite ill. We chatted for a while and when we parted I gave him a hug and kissed the side of his cheek. He felt stiff and awkward and I could tell that he found it hard to respond. However, his eyes were smiling as I left him so I didn't feel my spontaneous actions had been rejected. He died a week later. How glad I was that I had showed him that I cared about him. We never know when this might be the only opportunity we have to say or do those things that need to be done, or which reflect our feelings.

Of course there will be situations within the family where you are close and you know this. You would do anything to help each other and you feel there is no need to express all this in words. But wouldn't it be nice if a brother, sister, parent, or child did say, 'I do love you' just once in a while? You could say it too!

POSITIVE CHANGE

If you have a relationship with someone that needs positive change, or you need to say things you have avoided saying, you may like to use the following exercise. Read through it first, then when you are ready to do it, find a quiet place where you will not be interrupted. (If there's no place at home, sit in your car, or close your eyes and do it on a train journey, or lock yourself in the bathroom for ten minutes).

Exercise 4 – Positive change to improving a relationship

1   Close your eyes, relax and breathe deeply for a few minutes. Pay attention to your breathing, try to smooth out any jerkiness or unevenness; feel your chest gently rise and fall as you breathe in and out . . . Now mentally check over your body starting with your toes and feet; tilt your toes up towards your body, tense the muscles and then let go and relax. Do

the same now with your calf muscles and then your thigh muscles – tense for a few moments and then let go and relax. Imagine that your legs are as heavy as lead, so heavy you just don't want to lift them. Now pull in your tummy muscles, hold them . . . let go and relax. Next, breathe in very deeply, hold that breath for a few seconds and then breath out and relax. Now tense your shoulders and your neck muscles; again hold that position for a few moments before you drop your shoulders, let go and relax. Finally tense the muscles in your arms and hands, make your hand into two fists and hold on tightly for a few moments . . . now release all that tension, let go and relax.

2   For a few minutes pay attention to external sounds – maybe you can hear the sound of distant traffic or people going past. Now be aware of any closer sounds, the clock ticking, your own breathing.

3   Picture yourself in a place where you feel utterly at peace – make this somewhere out of doors, it could be in a lovely garden (real or imagined), a beautiful beach, in a woodland, sitting outside a country pub – anywhere will do.

4   As you picture yourself sitting there you begin to examine a relationship you want to improve. With no need to defend yourself or to feel negative emotions, just think about how you could improve this relationship. Move things around inside your head until you feel good about them – imagine a positive response.

5   Imagine that you now look up and see, coming toward you, the figure of that very person you have been thinking about. You wave and they wave back. Perhaps you rise and go to meet them. Minutes later you are sitting side by side, relaxed and peaceful.

6   You begin to talk, saying to them those things you have been needing to say, things that will really improve your relationship. You clear away old misunderstandings affixing no blame, accepting responsibility for improving the situation. You can tell this person how much you care, how important

they are to you. If it feels appropriate you can take their hand, give them a hug.

7 When you are able to envisage a positive response, make yourself a promise to follow it through when next you see this person – if necessary make a point of arranging a meeting – or just turn up on the doorstep with a smile.

The negative pictures we play over and over again inside our minds have a very powerful influence on the way we see life and the way we behave. By changing negative pictures to positive ones we change our responses.

LIVING WITH THE ELDERLY

Why is it that so many elderly people now live in nursing homes or retirement homes? If we go back fifty years they were almost unheard of. Five generations ago almost everyone's way of earning a living was connected with the land, but as industry developed, and cars, trains and planes enabled us to explore our world, many families were split up. People moved to find work, to get promotion, to cash in on new opportunities. They began to have choices so that some moved to live in the country and others settled in the cities making them their new home. As things progressed and ageing parents needed to be taken care of, or helped by living close to their families, there was, in many cases, no longer anyone to fill that role. Moving an elderly parent to live with you can work but it can also be quite disastrous. If they have lived most of their lives in one location, moving means leaving behind old friends and a way of life that has been familiar to them for perhaps seventy or eighty years. Caring for an elderly relative may inhibit other activities such as working on committees, or spending time with friends, or pursuing hobbies, and one can begin to feel very resentful. The elderly person in your life may be a delight to live with, but they could be cantankerous, bitter, ungrateful. If you are contemplating such a move, the best advice is to give it a try-out first. If this is impossible, think hard before you make any move that cannot be undone; it is kinder never to embark on such a project unless you absolutely know you can stick with it. Constant conflict or living with unpleasant undertones is not the way for the elderly to end their days.

Janet and her husband decided to take over the responsibility of caring for her mother. They built an annexe on to their house which enabled the old lady to have her own rooms and to be comfortable. After six months they had become desperate. The mother was so lonely that she spent every evening sitting with them and they almost completely lost the privacy in their relationship they had previously enjoyed. When they tried to explain this to her she retired to her rooms and refused to spend any time with them, eating alone and sitting for hours staring out of the window.

You going to be okay, granny?

To live with an elderly person can be very rewarding, adding another dimension to your life; perhaps they take on little tasks and actually afford you more freedom. But if they become very severely disabled or mentally confused, unless you have plenty of support, you can expect to feel exhausted and fed-up at times if not downright depressed. A lot of communication and fore-thought needs to go into the decision before you take a step that can be very hard to retract. If you are forced into placing your parent in a 'home', beware of guilt. Spending the next five years feeling remorse will do no one any good. Where you honestly cannot see living together working, it is better to avoid conflict by taking the right action from the beginning and then, recognizing why you have done this, you do not carry around a burden of guilt. Remember, you have done what you believe is best. Although families may love each other, it is not always possible, or advisable, for them to live together.

If you have an elderly person living with you and there is a lot of conflict or irritation, try to identify the core of the problem. It may be that you are not getting enough time to yourself. In this case seek help, there really is plenty out there. If you make it known to your local church they will probably be able to arrange for some 'sitters' to come and visit your old mum or dad. Help The Aged and The Carer's Group are two organizations that can offer practical help and advice. You are far less likely to get fed-up if you have time to pursue your own interests. Remember also that the elderly need to have friends and interests of their own; by helping to arrange this you enable them to retain their own identity and provide outside mental stimulus.

Julie had looked after her mother for two years without a break when she exploded one day, yelled at her mother, smacked her, and then burst into tears. It wasn't until all this happened that she realized she was at breaking point. It need never have happened if she had acknowledged her feelings earlier and taken steps to give herself time away.

TOTAL BREAKDOWN

When this occurs within a family it seems that nothing can ever resolve the situation. Even when attending a funeral of a close member of the family, those who have never spoken for years may still ignore each. Sadly, they miss the opportunity to move forward and let bygones be bygones.

Before any possible hope for reconciliation there must be a desire to put things right. This may only be on the part of one of the injured parties but can still be a positive starting point.

Alice was in this position, her daughter-in-law had not spoken to her for over ten years and neither had she seen her two grandchildren in all that time. Her son still visited her very occasionally but always alone. He never mentioned his family unless asked and then excused his children not visiting by explaining that they were too busy with their studies; he had to admit that his wife simply would not come. Alice said she didn't know why, but I believe that she was using denial as a way of protecting herself. Finally she decided that she would do anything, even say she was sorry for whatever had caused the rift, just to see her family again before it was too late. She was seventy-eight and realized that time may be running out. Alice tried communicating this to her son, asking him to relay it to her daughter-in-law, but there was never any response. We can empathize with the old lady, and also appreciate the impossible position the son was in – he couldn't force his wife to visit and maybe the children really didn't care about an old lady they hadn't seen in ten years. There is also the possibility that the wife refused to let the grandchildren visit and forcing the issue could have caused conflict within the marriage. But then we don't know what happened to cause the rift, we don't know what Alice said or did – or the way in which it was interpreted may have hurt the daughter-in-law. We can't judge. Let us hope we would have handled things differently.

A few months ago my son brought home for the night a young man who was backpacking around England. He had come from Australia and hadn't seen his father or paternal grandmother for almost twenty years. There had been a complete rift in the family following his father's return to England which resulted in the children being brought up in another country without any contact. Richard had decided it was time to put things right. He arrived on his grandmother's doorstep without any warning. The welcome he received had been overwhelming. In his own words, 'Just turning up had been the right thing to do.' Then Richard met his father, still filled with anger and resentment for the way he had abandoned the family and made no effort to keep in touch. But when Richard looked at his father those feelings melted away as he saw his father as 'a guy with a problem'. Richard told me: 'We had a wonderful reunion and a most memorable day. I still saw flashes of his temper that had scared me as a child, but they were no longer directed towards me – sometimes it happened with the traffic, once when he lost the parking space he was about to take. I actually felt sorry for him.'

We should use negative experiences as learning experiences, this way good can come from anything. In Richard's case he vowed never ever to abandon his family, no matter what happened. When he had talked with his father for some time he discovered that the reason his father had failed to keep in touch was that he had believed it would be better that way for all of them.

To grow up we do need to move away from our parents; we have to develop ways of survival that do not include them. However, we are part of a 'tribe' and contact is essential to our completeness. The disappearance of this close family contact is, I believe, one of the reasons why modern society is having such a hard time. The security, on-going values, the urge to care for the elderly, the community spirit, are all being lost and there is nothing to replace them.

HOMOSEXUALITY

An intimate relationship between two people of the same sex can cause all kinds of conflict, especially within the families of those two people. Although gay relationships are now much more freely talked about, most parents find it hard to understand how *their* child could become homosexual. The parents may feel that they and their values are being totally rejected. Before decrying their son's or daughter's behaviour out of hand, they need to find out more and to try and understand. Following detailed research it is now known that many homosexual men do actually have either a differently constructed brain or hormonal balance. Homosexual men rarely choose this path but are compelled there by the way they function. One client, in attempting to convey his own particular internal conflict told me, 'The way I feel has little to do with my sexual responses but in a hundred different ways I think and feel like a woman trapped in a man's body.' Both men and women who choose partners of the same sex as themselves may also have been influenced by traumas in their past that caused a certain psychological response. Lizzy, whose mother demanded to know why her daughter was in a lesbian relationship replied, 'Because you never loved me, mother.' In her own way she was seeking the love of another women to compensate for what she lacked as a child.

PROTECTION

I have recently been in contact with several families where one member is known to be taking drugs. Protecting them, supporting them financially, bailing them out, achieves nothing. 'But we can't let him go to prison – or starve,' one father said to me. The son is twenty-seven and still living at home.

Protection is instinctual and families, even those who have

considerable conflict, will close ranks against a common enemy. You may call your sister anything, but heaven help the stranger who dares to criticize her!

It takes immense strength to stand back and let those you care about answer for their own misdeeds. This, however, is often the best and kindest way to help them. Making excuses for them, justifying their unlawful or unacceptable behaviour, blaming others, does not resolve their problem. If you could see into a crystal ball you really wouldn't do it.

If conflict occurs, or is resident in your family, examine it carefully. Having decided that you really want to end it, proceed with the following exercise by first answering the questions and then making your decisions.

1   How long has it been going on? (If it persists longer than a day or two it needs your immediate attention.)
2   Do you know the root cause?
3   How important is the issue?
4   Do you understand the reactional response of the other person?
5   Do you understand why you are angry, upset?
6   No matter where the fault lies, are you prepared to say you are sorry without adding conditions to this in any way? (It's no use saying 'I'm sorry, but you did start it' – or 'I'm sorry, but if you hadn't . . .')
7   You have decided to end the conflict so you a) call a truce or agree to disagree and let it go or b) say you're sorry or c) forgive unconditionally.

Depending on the situation, you may choose to do one or all three of these.

There can be no *ifs* or *buts*, to bring conflict to an end the 'sorry' must be genuine and not conditional. It was suggested to a man who declared he really did want to make things up with his brother, to telephone this brother and simply said that he was sorry. 'But it wasn't my fault!' he declared. 'I didn't *cause* the rift.'

'But do you want to be friends again?' he was asked. The man's eyes filled with tears; he nodded. 'Then who was right or wrong two years ago doesn't even come into it. Just say you're sorry,' he was advised. It worked, the man returned ten minutes later beaming all over his face. 'Thanks,' he said. 'We're seeing each other next week. You can't believe how pleased he was to hear me.'

There is the possibility that when you try to put things right you will be rejected or verbally abused, but you will have tried and that has to be worth the risk. If you approach the other person with an open mind and your intention is to show that you care and that the person is important to you, this usually gets a positive response.

I have a friend who regularly tries to communicate with her estranged sister; to date it hasn't worked. This doesn't step Peggy from trying. 'You never know,' she says, 'perhaps, one day she will want to be friends again, but if I give up trying there isn't even a chance.' In the meantime she prays for the happiness and well-being of that sister.

Prayer, or meditative thought, is a way of mentally transmitting positive vibrations. How often have you thought of someone you haven't spoken to in months (maybe years) and they phone or you receive a letter from them? All thought is a form of energy – it has an effect.

5 Friends and Neighbours

We expect our friends to understand us. They have been specially chosen, not thrust upon us through family relationships, or forced into our lives by our working environment. The relationship with friends ought to be ideal, so why do conflicts happen? How can hurtful words and insults arise between friends? Why do friends so often seem to disappoint us or let us down? And how can we nurture a friendship?

Our attitude, as we have already seen, is shaped by our experiences. If we have been let down in the past we may convey negative messages and our reserve or mistrust may be misunderstood or misinterpreted. Self-doubt or resentment begins to creep in: *Is it me, or them?*

EXPECTATION

Expectation also plays a large part in the quality of our friendship and relationships with neighbours. Who gives and who takes? Are your expectations too high? Too idealistic? Do you mis-interpret the behaviour of others, look for slights or react adversely to criticism? Criticism can be hurtful and destructive, but when offered by a friend – the one person you can really trust – you should be able to examine it and see how it can be effectively utilized. Someone who cares about you is not going to wilfully offer destructive criticism.

Jill is a friend whom Jackie sees about four times a year. They

We need to get our priorities right

speak on the phone in-between times and enjoy the same hobbies and interests. It occurred to Jill recently that she hadn't heard from her friend for some time. When she mentioned this to a member of the family it was pointed out to her that she was always the one who made contact. 'Perhaps,' they suggested, 'she doesn't really want to see you or keep in touch.' This had never occurred to Jill, neither had she noticed that she was the one who always phones. For a few moments doubt wrapped dark fingers around her mind. Was she pushing a friendship that was over? Why did she keep in touch with her? Well, she admitted to herself, I am very fond of her and I enjoy her company. Jill made a decision and dialled her number. Jackie sounded delighted to hear her. 'How come you never ring me?' Jill asked. 'Well, you are always so busy,' Jackie explained. 'I know you'll get in touch when you have time so I leave it to you.'

Bringing things out in the open, asking without accusing, being optimistic about the outcome, can all help to avoid misunderstandings and arguments.

Sometimes friendship may be spoiled by feelings of jealousy. If you had to share parents with a number of competing siblings all after parental attention, then it is easy to see why you may want a 'special friend' all to yourself.

Close friendship should give room for self-expression. Often possessiveness occurs when you have only one friend and you see him or her equally enjoying the company of several others. Suddenly you don't feel so special any more. You may look for confirmation of your doubts and begin to read all kinds of things into their behaviour: they haven't rung you for a fortnight, they ignored you at the last party, they belittled you in front of others.

We cannot hold on to a friendship by strangling it. The relationship needs freedom to breathe. Show that you care, even tell your friend how special she is to you, but don't make her feel guilty about other friends or you will soon find them avoiding you. If you are having these kinds of problems you need to expand your own group of friends, start a new hobby, mix with a different group, offer your help to a charity. No one need be lonely or friendless, but we do have to give to receive and in this case one needs to give of oneself and one's time.

There is the danger of trying to fit in with a valued friend's expectations rather than being oneself. If, for example, you value time spent with your friend but really don't enjoy outdoor sport you ought to be able to explain this and to step back and not mind when they enjoy that pastime with someone else. This also applies to intimate relationships.

JUDGING OTHERS

Where there is complete trust between friends you can say or do almost anything, knowing it will not be misinterpreted. You are within your rights to firmly defend friends against unfair criticism and gossip.

When Pat left her husband and two children the whole village was talking – how could she do such a thing? 'They were such lovely children,' everyone said, 'and the husband had given her everything.' Pat was a neighbour of mine, I knew her well, and when she left without telling anyone I was convinced that she must have a very good reason. There was no way she would have left her children unless something absolutely terrible had forced her to go. I even began to wonder whether she had been kidnapped or murdered. I waited. Six months later she got in touch. It was then I discovered that her husband had become physically violent towards her, though she had never mentioned this before. She also told me that he had threatened to kill both her and the children if she tried to take them away from him. Pat had made the only decision she felt possible at that time.

This poses the question do we ever have the right to judge another? Do we *really* know the facts and what goes on in someone else's life?

It is easy sometimes to push a friendship too far, to have unrealistic expectations, or to presume that they would do as much for us. Sometimes this isn't possible, for we all have our own way of evaluating things and coping. Being able to drop everything to help a friend may come easily to some, but there are other people who get easily stressed and find several commitments arriving at the same time too much for them. However, this doesn't make them less of a friend. Judging other people by the way *you* would have acted can be very dangerous and often unfair. *I would never have done (or said) that . . .* is a response prompted by the belief that others ought to behave as you would.

Remember friendship is invaluable, tend it with care and when necessary, give your friend the benefit of the doubt. Never take friendships for granted.

NEIGHBOURS

Unless we live in isolation, most of us have to learn to live in close proximity to other people. Even if you never speak to the man down the street or the people next door, neighbours can still cause an awful lot of havoc in your life. We have all heard of noisy neighbours who have their hi-fi blasting out music into the early hours of the morning; screaming children out in the street when one is trying to study; the man who decides his hedge needs trimming and hacks yours at the same time. Conflict with neighbours affects most of us at some time during our lives.

Learning to use certain strategies and skills will help to avoid conflict and confrontation. Understanding how to interpret body language can prevent aggressive reactions from escalating out of control.

Situations with neighbours sometimes just cannot be ignored and one can't sell up and move on every time there is a problem. So how do we cope with conflicting situations with neighbours? Of course the best way is to try to prevent conflict occurring in the first place. Try to be a good neighbour. Develop a caring attitude with a willingness to see both points of view. We need to appreciate when someone is having a stressful time and to make allowances. Remember that it is not the offending behaviour that usually causes the problem but how it is discussed: a polite request to speak about the problem that is causing you distress or irritation can often result in it being resolved when you try co-operatively to find a solution. If your approach results in withdrawal, the neighbour avoids you and does nothing about the situation, it may be his way of dealing with what he sees as unreasonable demands, or something about which he can do nothing – his son coming home late at night and revving his motorbike engine under your window, or his cat digging up your plants.

Sometimes finding a solution can be fun. Mark kept his dog chained up in the yard at night. The problem was that Mark slept overnight at his parents house in town on Fridays which resulted in the dog howling until the early hours of the morning. Mark refused to do anything about the situation. Frustrated neighbours had tried complaining but it made no difference. They discussed ways of resolving the problem; everything from poisoning the dog to opening the gate and letting it out was suggested. Then someone had the bright idea of dropping a large marrow bone over the fence each Friday night. This kept the dog happy for hours and peace once more returned to the community.

Driven beyond reason we tend to resort to yelling or even physical violence. Neighbours can end up in the courts because things have got out of control and neither party knew when to retreat or when to give the situation time to cool down. When yelling doesn't work one may retreat into silence, steadfastly ignoring the man or woman next door, behaving as if they are not there. This can cause a lot of anger in those being treated as if they don't exist and a kind of hatred campaign gets underway. All this may sound extreme and you may think that this would never happen to you, but it is surprising how certain things can drive a normally quiet, law-abiding person to take things into their own hands or to violate decent civilized behaviour. A newcomer to the district is often viewed as having less rights than those who have been there for years and any 'pushy' or authoritative behaviour may be met with resentment.

The most recent research finds inconsiderate parking as being the most frequent cause of friction between neighbours. Now wouldn't you think a thing like that could be easily resolved?

Continuing to be a kind or thoughtful neighbour, despite provocation, can sometimes work miracles. Jack had such an experience.

Jack bought land which had a public footpath running through one field. Months later he decided to plough up the land and re-seed it as it was in a very poor state.

A woman, who always took her dog into the field for exercise, complained bitterly to him: 'You have no right to do this, all the villagers have been coming here for years,' she protested.

'But the field needed ploughing,' he tried to explain.

She didn't want to listen. 'Remember, we were here long before you came. You have to live amongst us,' she warned him. 'You had better watch out.'

Well, Jack re-seeded his field, put up new styles and re-established the path. He often saw the woman out with her dog, walking the path across his land – she consistently ignored him.

Then he heard that her husband had died. Despite her rudeness he felt sorry for her and found himself wondering how she was going to manage on her own.

The next time he saw her he made a point of stopping her. 'Sorry to hear about your husband. If you need a lift into town any time I always take my wife in on Fridays to shop and we could pick you up if it would help.'

Putting the past behind them, they began regularly to give her a lift and the woman's life was enriched by knowing two such lovely people.

Sometimes it takes a tragedy to get things back into perspective and to recognize what really matters in life. Often being right or wrong simply isn't important.

Refusing to get directly involved leaves no possible way to resolve a conflict. It does, however, enable some people to feel better as the heartbeat slows and one feels more relaxed and in control than when one is constantly in the 'battlefield'.

In circumstances involving conflict with neighbours, research has shown that it is men who admit to wanting to avoid confrontation while women seek actively to 'sort things out'. This is where women may prod and push a man into a situation he would much rather avoid. *You'll have to speak to him; you're going to have to do something; you can't let them walk all over you*, are the kind of phrases that can push someone into endless argu-ments or confrontation. If you truly feel that your way of dealing with things by doing nothing is the wisest course of action, stick to it. The problem is that by doing so you can end up feeling badly about yourself, in which case you need to remind yourself that the person pushing you may not have the best of intentions. To avoid a row or fight doesn't mean you are weak, insignificant, or a coward. Sometimes backing off is the wisest thing to do, and the bravest.

An archetypal figure can create conflict that seems totally unreasonable. If someone, whom you really hardly know, creates feelings of fear or mistrust in you, it may be that their appearance, or voice, is reminding you of a fearsome teacher or father who always intimidated you. In a case like this you are going to find it hard to respond to that person without prejudice. If, for no apparent reason, you find yourself disliking or distrusting a neighbour, ask yourself if he reminds you of someone from your past. Once you have recognized why you are experiencing such an irrational response you will find it easier to accept that person without prejudging.

DIFFUSING A SITUATION

First of all we need to recognize that using a certain posture or words can demean, insult, suggest criticism and alienate people. To diffuse a volatile situation both your words and body language are important. To say you are sorry while adopting a threatening stance will be interpreted as tactics to get the other person off their guard while you come in for the 'kill'. At least 70 per cent of communication is body language, your words may deceive but your actions will tell the true story. So when you try to diffuse an escalating argument you must be true to what you think.

Avoid argument wherever possible, it prevents you thinking clearly, creates a reaction instead of a response, and causes most people to move into either a defensive or attacking position. What you need, to make things work, is *communication not argument.*

If the neighbour's radio is persistently blasting out at midnight and preventing you from sleeping, explain what your problem is, don't verbally attack him as a thoughtless moron. Give the other person a graceful way to retract by suggesting that perhaps they were not aware that . . .

However, if someone is in a rage and threatening your life, you back off. No attempt to negotiate at that moment is going to work. Enraged people are incapable of applying reason. You may try at another time, use an independent person, write a letter or try a phone call, but at that moment you need to remove yourself from the scene.

When a situation is heading for long-term conflict you may need to ask yourself:

- Can I afford to let this go? If it isn't going to cause you to have a breakdown, intrude on your space, cost you a lot in monetary terms, letting go may be the simplest path to a peaceful existence.
- Is there any way I can help this situation? Often, by doing something that is seen as helpful you get the co-operation you have been seeking.
- Would it be better to use an independent person to help resolve this?
- Is legal action necessary? Remember it's costly and there is no guarantee that you will win.
- Do they need to feel that they have won, and if so, can I arrange this while still achieving my goal? I found this approach once worked very well with me when, by allowing a neighbour to purchase a piece of land he had coveted for some time I was able to purchase the land alongside his property which he had tried to 'protect' at all costs, even though it did not officially belong to him. He was, I discovered, afraid that if it changed hands it would encroach on his privacy. What happened in the end was that we agreed between us to see that this never happened and he became most helpful and co-operative.

Megan came to see me as a client explaining that she was suffering from terrible depression.

'I never feel well any more,' she told me, 'and I'm always depressed.'

I asked her to try to identify when all this started. Gradually she told me of a new neighbour who had moved in next door and, after only a few weeks, had hacked down a hedge that was extremely old and rare.

Tears flowed as she sobbed, 'It was such a beautiful hedge. How could he have done it? And half of it came into our garden. The trouble is that the roots were his side of the fence and so we can't take legal action.'

'How do you think legal action would have helped?' I queried.

'It might have stopped him doing anything like that again.'

It might, but it wouldn't replace the hedge she was grieving over. I then suggested that she considered the best thing she thought she could do in the situation.

'Move,' she replied. 'I can't bear to look at the man. But we can't afford to.'

Here was a situation where a compromise had to be found. Of course she could go on living there feeling miserable and upset, or she could make some positive decisions that would enable her to feel better. She wasn't ready yet to forgive him.

I suggested planting a new hedge her side of the fence – one that she could tend and watch grow to maturity.

'But first,' I said, 'why not go round to see him, express calmly how much you cared about the hedge. You might even suggest that perhaps he didn't know how rare and beautiful it was when it flowered. Then you could ask his co-operation in seeing that your new hedge was allowed to grow happily on your side of the fence.'

Before she was able to do this I saw her several times, helping her to build confidence by using positive affirmation and visualizing a satisfactory outcome.

Once she had a clear picture in her mind of the new hedge she went to call on the man next door.

'How did it go?' I asked when she next came to see me.

'Oh, he was really ever so nice. He explained that the hedge was scratching his car every time he drove in, and he didn't know about the hedge flowering.'

Her smile told me the problem had been resolved.

UNDERPRIVILEGED

Badly behaved neighbours may have a problem that is reflected in the way they treat you but actually has nothing directly to do with you. I speak of those who feel underprivileged. This may be in materialistic terms, educationally, in appearance, culture or background. Much of school bullying is as a result of young people feeling in some way underprivileged; by attacking they are suggesting the fault is the other person's. You could label this envy. Whatever the reason, the build up of resentment needs an outlet and they are going to take it out on someone. If you have a nice car and the family down the road cannot afford one, it is quite possible they may let down your tyres or 'accidentally' scratch the side of your car. It isn't just the car that causes this behaviour but the fact that they feel deprived and angered by a situation they believe is not their fault and they want to hit out at somebody.

Remember that at a fundamental level we are tribal, and being part of a tribe offers protection. This is why underprivileged people often form into gangs or groups, it gives them support and enables them to feel safe. You are hardly likely to take on, or to remonstrate with someone who has just trampled all over your garden while searching for a ball if there are twenty other youngsters standing at the gate. Sometimes it is better to retreat. Then again, sometimes it needs someone only to give them a chance and to treat them with courtesy to get a positive response. Make a person feel good about themselves, give them a chance, and they almost always respond positively.

SUFFERING

Almost daily our attention is drawn to stories of suffering: from the old gentleman who lives up the road losing his wife, to innocent people imprisoned, chained, starved and kept in total darkness. The stories that the people concerned tell us are, in themselves, a surprise, for they speak of their learning from those experiences: that wonderful moment when rays of sunlight pierced the dark, or the discovery of a new insight into love. I wonder, does it take something so extreme to happen before we learn to get life into perspective? When you consider many of the things we argue about or allow to contaminate our thinking, declaring that we will never forget or forgive, we ought to be ashamed. But things that are close to home and immediate have such a powerful effect on our emotions that it is more difficult to be compassionate than when things do not affect us personally.

My friend, Pam, who died some years ago, held the belief that most of the things we allowed to upset us were really just little things. This meant she would clean up after a neighbour who had trimmed the hedge and allowed the trimmings to fall on her side of the fence. 'After all,' she reasoned, 'he did cut the hedge.' Quietly putting things right can often take very little effort and save unnecessary conflict.

Feelings are very powerful, they do count, and there are those who carry around so much hurt that it damages their whole life. So when it is 'only a little thing', learning to let it go is the sensible way to prevent the building, brick by brick, of a wall of pain based on small differences.

Let's end the conflict and meet halfway, is now being adopted by nations in an attempt to avoid further war and bloodshed. It is called negotiation. The same attitude could prevent fights or stony silences with our neighbours. What is really important is resolving the problem, not winning the argument.

Tips

- Respect at all times your neighbours' rights to their own opinions and values.
- Try to be a good neighbour.
- When a conflicting situation arises, stick to the issue not who is right or wrong.

- Be courteous.
- Recognize when a discussion is turning into an argument and suggest you leave it until another specified time.
- If you can keep the issue impersonal it will help – you will not be seen as attacking the person but dealing with what has happened.
- When you know that you are in the wrong, admit it and apologize.

6   Conflict in the Workplace

In my research, questions covering the subject of conflict at work prompted the most response. People seemed always willing to answer my queries, throw in their own suggestions, and explain how and why they believed conflict arose.

Those things employees listed as the cause of most conflict in the workplace included:

- lack of communication about what has to be done and what is going on
- bosses who really don't know what they are talking about
- colleagues who don't pull their weight
- bosses who don't pull their weight
- bosses who won't listen
- colleagues who will never do anything to help outside their specific job
- being unfairly blamed and given no chance to explain or defend oneself
- refusing to take responsibility
- unfair criticism and accusations
- bosses expecting too much from the employee
- undervalued – lack of recognition and praise
- unreasonable expectations
- preferential treatment
- rumours that come about due to lack of proper information
- ideas that are put into operation without evidence that they will work
- silly rules and pettiness

- over-zealous management
- hypocrisy
- sexism and conflict arising from sexual differences and behaviour

From the management point of view problems included:

- unco-operative staff
- people who believe certain jobs are beneath them
- employees who down tools and always leave on time no matter how acute a problem may be
- ignoring priorities
- not completing work on time and failing to inform
- changes in law and legislation that have to be implemented but appear unreasonable to staff
- people who allow petty quarrels to affect their work
- people who put their personal lives first
- partners, co-directors and co-managers who refuse to co-operate or implement work that has to be done, fail to successfully delegate, have different priorities, do not make themselves clear

When I asked about conflict with customers and clients I was told that those kind of problems were much easier to resolve as there was usually a willingness on both sides to achieve a satisfactory outcome.

Depending on whether you are the boss or the staff, problems are viewed differently. One man I know, who has experienced both positions, thought that bosses who won't listen, preferential treatment, people who put their personal lives first, and a negative attitude were for him, the worst.

He shared with me his philosophy: I enjoy my work, do the best I can, never quit when things get difficult, and I take the time to enjoy my hobbies and interests.

I recall one managing director of a very large engineering business telling me that having hobbies which he treated with as

Little things can drive you crazy

much enthusiasm as he did work, was what kept him sane. His commitment to running the local junior football team meant that no matter where he was during the week, he was always home for the match on Saturday. 'Those boys are our future,' he told me. 'One day, the respect we show to them now will be reflected in how they handle life when they are grown up.'

RECOGNIZING PRIORITIES

The most important thing in the workplace is getting the job done. If this fails everyone is out of a job anyway. People who fight against change sometimes fail to appreciate this. What seems unnecessary to them is often done to enable a business to survive or move forward. Sometimes there will have to be a complete restructure or the business goes under.

In some impossible situations the employer may decide that all the aggravation isn't worth the returns and close down the business. This happened some years ago with a man who had really tried very hard to care for the well-being of his employees. He had, at his own cost, arranged for them to receive full pay for up to three months when they were sick, private health treatment, paid time-off for further training, and at Christmas he went round to each home with a hamper of food and a turkey. When unrest and resistance began among his workers because a full order book meant working overtime, he felt things had gone far enough. He closed the business and retired. 'I have made enough to live if I am careful,' he said. 'I just couldn't take any more. It wasn't worth it.'

It helps if you work in an organization, or a large firm, to recognize that the most successful way of accomplishing things is to drop the 'them and us' attitude and to see yourselves as part of a complete unit. You need each other to make things work. You also, in many cases, need the investors, so if a large proportion of the profits goes in their direction it helps to bear in mind that without their investment there wouldn't be a job.

It is important to recognize that people's beliefs differ. This doesn't necessarily mean that one is wrong and the other right – they are very different. We may have different beliefs from our colleagues, or staff, but that should not prevent a joint effort from succeeding when our objectives are the same.

Where people's personalities differ it is not possible to change them, so learning to work with them is the only way. Seeing things differently at times may turn out to be a real bonus.

Your personal aims will not always coincide with those of the people with whom you work. We need to recognize when this is the case and so avoid disappointment or frustration. There will always be those for whom family commitments or hobbies come first. Insisting on overtime being worked and failing to appreciate the importance of family celebrations or a local football match, will not get you the best results – it could lose you a good worker or colleague.

However, you need also to be aware of the dangers in getting too personally involved, or you can find that you become a welfare officer for the whole family of your staff – wasting precious hours on the phone trying to help resolve problems that ought not to concern you as an employer. You can, at times, become too kind and sympathetic which is fine in your own time but doesn't help run a business.

The most important thing from the management's point of view is completing the job and getting the work out so that it can be invoiced. As an employee you may feel that quality is more important and that you cannot bear to see work for which you are responsible go out if it's not up to standard. As you are paid by those who employ you, then you may have to accept that in the workplace some of your standards or priorities have to take second place. The stress of being forced to put into production new inventions before they were ready caused a friend of mine to become ill. Finally he decided he was not going to compromise and so left the firm. Life is about making decisions and from time-to-time we all have to make them.

Fix your mind on the goal, remember why you are working and if you are unfulfilled try talking to someone who may be able to help. Perhaps you need more responsibility, flexibility or a new challenge.

Your personal goals may be quite different from your firm's. Can you live with this? Perhaps your dreams and ideals will need to be realized away from the workplace. People divide roughly into two categories where their work is involved: there are those to whom the work they do gives their life purpose and meaning, and there are those who work to earn the money which allows them to do what they wish with their lives elsewhere. If these two can be combined there is a total sense of fulfilment but for most people this is not possible.

Cassie works night shifts and long hours because by working this way her income is greater and that enables her to pursue her hobby which is water-skiing. This hobby means so much to her that she is prepared to put up with anti-social hours and dirty, physical hard work. She still does her best but does not delude herself by attempting to clothe it with high ideals.

If you do not like your job you have three choices: leave, change your attitude, or accept you don't like it and focus on the advantages: perhaps it's close to home and does not involve long journeys; or it enables you to finish when the children come out of school; or the money is good.

FOR THOSE IN AUTHORITY

Tips to improve relationships and efficiency:

- Avoid being patronizing.
- Beware of taking people for granted.
- Do not make promises you have no intention of fulfilling. (*We'll see about that* is often interpreted as a promise).
- When you make mistakes don't use other people to cover up for you.
- Take time to get to know your staff.
- Beware of those who focus only on the problems and not on the solutions.
- If something isn't working, change it. When you discover an old way was more productive don't be too proud to admit it, and reinstate the practice or procedure.
- When changes are about to take place that will affect the staff keep them informed.
- When you set deadlines follow them through – if they are seen as not important, staff will lose trust and confidence in you.
- Remember it's okay to point out when things are not going according to plan or drop below standard so long as you also give praise when it is justified.
- Recognize where your responsibility begins and ends: to take on more than you can handle leads to inefficiency, to pass things on to someone else when the going gets tough is unfair, especially when you are directly responsible.

- Act with dignity, treat others with courtesy, apply a little humour, and with a bit of luck you'll survive. No one said that being at the top would be easy!

A man who was in charge of the firm where my husband worked always made a point of walking through the workshops once a week – no matter how busy he was – and speaking with each employee in turn. He would keep a little notebook to remind him when someone had been on holiday, or celebrated an important occasion, or a baby was expected, and his kind enquiries were always appreciated. My husband told me that any member of the staff would have done anything for that man, he was so well-liked and respected. *He showed that he cared.*

In a conflicting situation, being a good listener will reduce stress and lead to better communication. People need to feel they are being taken seriously and even if nothing can be done to alter a situation you will have more co-operation if they feel you have at least heard them out.

BLAME

The role of management is to skipper the ship and make sure that the crew are looked after and that you arrive safely at your destination. It is absolutely no use blaming one of the crew when the ship is going down, so be aware at all times of your true responsibility. To many, injustice is the hardest thing to accept. As the boss, proving you did not do something, or that it wasn't your fault, is something you may have to let go. Seen in this light you are going to have to take most of the responsibility, criticism, and blame when things do not go well.

As we have already seen, accusation fails to get a positive response; where this concerns more than one person those concerned immediately join ranks to defend themselves. Intentional or not, by accusing someone you cause them to feel threatened. Try to convey the feeling that you really do want to find the solution rather than blame anyone. *You make me angry* is an incorrect statement – we choose our responses either consciously or unconsciously. Also remember that to blame someone else is to render yourself helpless, for what you are saying is that you can't do anything about the situation because of someone or something. When things go wrong your approach needs to be NOT *Who is responsible?* but *How did this happen? How can we correct it? How can we prevent it happening again?*

Instead of searching for someone to blame, learn to see that sometimes all that is needed is to forgive and accept responsibility. We all make wrong decisions sometimes, whether you are the President of America or the person who opens the mail. When a thing is done it cannot be undone; by applying a positive approach you move on. Making mistakes, doing something wrong, is a learning experience – you know not to do it that way next time.

All too often our responses are governed by fear. *Will they sack me? Bawl me out? Make me look ridiculous in front of everyone? Will I have to pay for this?*

To resolve the problem where blame is being used, even if this involves only two people, calling a meeting (or enquiry) is a good way of temporarily removing yourself from face to face conflict. It gives both of you space and time to consider, and although deliberate delay can also cause conflict, it is more often constructive in helping ultimately to resolve the problem. 'Let's meet after lunch – or tomorrow – and take a look at this. We will both be in a better position to discuss it rationally.' If you have the authority to give the meeting an official air this will also help. It may also prevent things going that far another time.

Many people are currently using the media as an excuse and blaming the bad examples of well-known personalities and misinformation. We blame TV or the newspapers for our problems or weaknesses. We are told that the reason we can't do certain things is because of the inability of teachers or the police or politicians to set an example – or that our diet, pollution or a strange new virus is the cause of our problems. The trouble lies in the fact that at least half of the time we really believe what we are being told. It used to be called propaganda, now perhaps it would be more accurate to label it 'systematic destruction of the human being's ability to think for himself'.

Returning to the effects of delay: when you are waiting for some materials, a piece of equipment, or for a job to be done, excessive delay can be very serious. If nothing happens to right the situation, feelings will escalate from frustration to anxiety and then to anger. We have all heard people yelling abuse over the telephone when something like this happens. If your pipes burst and the plumber doesn't arrive, or all your lights have gone out and you are plunged into darkness, it is hard to stay calm. But really being politely insistent will get the man to your door faster than calling him names. If you are the person responsible for the delay – or misunderstanding – apologize, then excuse yourself and deal with the problem.

Waiting to be paid, especially if you run a small business, can eventually turn distress into outright anger. When polite requests fail and the customer ignores you, there becomes an explosive moment when you may feel like breaking down their door. Should you find yourself in this position it is more productive to let the small claims court deal with the problem.

EXCUSES

Excuses only irritate – if you are already stressed they can infuriate. Why do people use excuses? Usually to avoid admitting their omissions, weaknesses, faults, or to play for time. Excuses also enable us to avoid making the effort. One of the times when this most frequently occurs is when something or someone is late arriving.

Some people are habitually late and really just don't seem to know how to change. This can cause chaos within a family, frustration in a relationship, it may result in losing one's job at work. Someone with this problem needs retraining, step by step, by someone who has patience and understanding and who will offer support and encouragement. Sometimes a big shock, such as the one my mother once gave to my father, may work. Although my father had his own business, he always found getting up in the morning extremely difficult and depended on my mother to keep prodding him and nagging him until he finally got out of bed. Even then he grumbled at her and was not grateful. One morning she decided she'd had enough and left him sleeping. On waking he discovered he had missed a very important meeting. My mother refused to accept responsibility any longer and from then onwards he was forced to set the alarm clock and rise without any prompting.

Another type of person may have the completely opposite problem, always arriving far too early everywhere, which can be frustrating for those who are forced to fit into an unrealistic time schedule. At the root of this behaviour is fear. In Jenny's case, as a child, her mother's casual approach to time meant that Jenny was frequently late for school and had to walk into class amidst the whispers and giggles of classmates and the strident accusing voice of the teacher. Once Jenny identified the cause of her fear she was able to use a more realistic approach to being on time.

When you are tempted to use an excuse in your workplace, make sure it is a *reason* – you'll get a better response and won't experience guilt.

MAKING THINGS BETTER

No matter what your position at work, you can influence things for the better. Someone who is feeling very despondent can be smiling minutes later if the right approach is used. Happy people are more content, less likely to complain or get into arguments, and they create positive energy from which everyone benefits. Try smiling and sharing a joke with people who have really boring fruitless jobs. The fact that you bothered to notice them makes them suddenly aware that life isn't really so bad.

Remember to be aware of internal dialogue and tell yourself regularly that you're good at what you do; that work can be a real challenge; that your efforts do make a difference; and that you can make things happen – if you really want to.

If there is a bad atmosphere in the office where you work, or in the store, the ward, the classroom, on the workshop floor, look out for resentment – it isn't always towards the management. Where some workers appear to get off lightly while others carry the load there will be unrest and negative undercurrents. Again, you need to talk about it and see if anything can be done to improve the situation.

PETTINESS AND SILLY RULES

No matter how mature your outlook, pettiness or silly rules can get to you. Even if you maintain a calm outward appearance you can end up feeling very fed-up on the inside. Sometimes these feelings finally escalate into a frustrated explosion. Often those responsible are not aware that their decisions are causing negative reactions, or they are too obstinate to change them. Being told, 'You must not use the premises for personal activities' meant one woman being sacked because she operated a small lottery syndicate during the lunch hour in her own time. Another lady I know went to work at a checkout in a large food store. She was told that she mustn't pause to speak to other members of the staff still working on the tills when she stopped to go for her breaks. 'I have never treated people like that in my life!' she said, and a few days later gave in her notice.

You will probably have experienced petty rules yourself. If they bother you, try to communicate with the one responsible; it's possible that she is unaware of how pointless or infuriating the rules are. Maybe she can offer you a good reason for them that enables you to feel better about adhering to them.

People at management level who become over-zealous –

watching for every tiny misdemeanour – are focusing their attention in the wrong direction and will be seen as petty and small-minded. Saving a few pence while pounds are being wasted elsewhere happens all too frequently.

At a local motorway services the manager decided that in order to economize he would get rid of the man whose job it was to collect the overnight parking fee from lorry drivers. The man's wage was less than a quarter of what they took in fees but this was completely overlooked. When this was pointed out by one of the staff the information was ignored. Someone was either a very poor manager or on an ego trip that prevented him from admitting when he was wrong or that there might be a better way of doing things. Behaving like this does cause resentment and when a bigger issue comes up it may be used to fuel feelings of frustration that can then escalate into outright conflict.

The good news is that many organizations now recognize that useful information can be gleaned by listening to their staff and regular meetings are arranged for this reason. The person experienced in doing the job often knows more than the manager and can offer productive suggestions to improving quality, saving costs, or boosting output. Some firms even offer financial rewards to employees who put forward ideas for improving production or the product.

Unnecessary procedures and paperwork are also seen as stupid bureaucracy preventing people from getting on with their job. Blame here is usually justified and the government is beginning to recognize (at last!) that what people need is less paper work not more. It has been suggested that for some, creating more paperwork is a way of justifying their job – if this is true it does nothing for their self-esteem. In order to induce change, many people will have to speak out – certainly doctors, police and teachers I have listened to, bemoan the fact that they waste valuable time filling in sheets of paper that prevent them from doing the job they are employed to do. Such seemingly pointless requirements create frustration, feelings of impotence, and results in the build-up of stress. If you can do nothing to change the system it's best just to accept it or try to disregard that particular area – seething over it will do you no good at all.

UNREASONABLE RULES

A doctor recently expressed to me how unreasonable rules and requirements by the Government and within the health service were creating problems and causing stress in many medical practices. One major problem, he explained, was that in selecting doctors to join the practice (or to work in hospitals) they were not allowed to discriminate between the sexes. But in reality having an even balance of male and female doctors did not work. The female doctors, quite rightly, wanted to take time off to have a family, or to be with their family, and the majority wished to work only part-time. 'I'm all for fairness,' he said, 'but this doesn't work. It means that the rest of us have to work many extra hours to cover for up to six months at a time while a female doctor is taking maternity leave, and something like eighty per cent of night calls in our practice are done by the male doctors.' He wasn't belittling the contribution female doctors made, stating that many patients preferred to see a lady doctor. The only way to avoid this kind of stress and conflict, he believed, was to make sure that the requirements of the job were clearly defined and understood by all those concerned before *any* new doctor was taken into the practice.

The police force experiences similar problems with inflexible rules that prevent them from doing their job properly. If one policeman steps out of line in a volatile confrontation with a criminal by using swear words or hitting the culprit, he can be subjected to media exposure and criticism regardless of the circumstances. Quite recently a policeman who had been injured and was lying on the side of the road waiting for an ambulance used a swear word when speaking to a colleague. This was over-heard by a passer-by who reported him to the superintendent who then *had* to follow this up and use disciplinary action. Is it any wonder that such rules cause conflict?

Talking to a man who runs a small post office I discovered that impractical requirements and rules control his working life. For example, when someone wants to post a parcel the post office staff are supposed to weigh the parcel and then hand it back to the customer who must stick the stamps on himself. This, he pointed out, is almost impossible to do when they are busy as it means holding up everyone else while this takes place, or for the customer to move away while someone else is attended to and then to queue again to hand back in the parcel. Completing the paperwork for Recorded Delivery is also supposed to be done by the customer, but, as John told me, with his experience it is much more efficient for him to complete the paper work for them.

If you have any influence over rules which could be petty or unfair, perhaps you would listen to those affected, use common-sense, and *do something about them*. If you are the one affected, and no one will listen, it may help to turn those petty rules into cartoons in your head and see them as ridiculous even though you may have to follow them. This will help. Laughter is a wonderful way of coping with situations which you cannot change and it can also discharge negative energy. You may have had a personal experience of being in conflict with a colleague and then something happens that makes you both laugh, after that it's almost impossible to take the issue seriously.

RUMOURS

These are going to happen no matter how correct or careful you are. They can cause a great deal of mischief or upset. Start muttering that the firm is struggling and people begin to look for alternative employment. It is important to keep staff informed and by acting positively, to give them confidence. Some changes may have to be kept secret until implemented. If you are in this type of situation, demonstrate confident behaviour – remember that body language is constantly being read. When you are feeling excited, confident, or despairing, your staff will sense your mood.

When people become unsure they experience fear, and when people are afraid there is a build up of tension; often this tension is released by starting an argument. This can be prevented by *communicating effectively* and setting the right example.

Rumours at a personal level can easily degenerate into bickering, resentment and direct confrontation. If you hear rumours that concern you, before getting upset, investigate.

Bill, who is area manager of about twenty camera shops, heard that a letter had arrived on his superior's desk accusing him of racism. He was not only angry about this but also upset as he definitely did not see himself as a racist. Because he had not been informed directly of this letter he didn't feel he could do anything about it. However, distressing thoughts continued to bother him, he became distracted at work and his level of competence dropped. Finally he decided to ask his boss whether there was any truth in the rumour, and to explain his position, making it clear that he treated everyone on merit. As shop manager he was responsible for recruiting, and as almost half the staff were people of ethnic origin he felt he had evidence to support his position. He was delighted and relieved to hear his boss confirm that he had received such a report but had taken no action as he didn't believe a word of it.

Avoid spreading gossip. Before passing it on, ask yourself, *Am I right to talk about this?* If it is directed at you and is serious, the sooner you denounce it and/or ask those responsible to prove it, the better. Gossip and rumours can have a disastrous effect and even cause some people to take their own lives.

HYPOCRISY

Don't be a hypocrite. Telling your staff that there is a need to economize and then going out and buying a new car isn't going to convey the right message. As we have seen with people in recently privatized public utilities, managers giving themselves large salary increases while freezing the spending budget or cutting back on staff only creates resentment and loss of respect.

'Say what you mean and stick by what you say' is a good way of avoiding this problem. People do respect sincerity, and by being honest and sincere you earn a positive response.

When the boss of a small factory went down on the workshop floor to help get out an important consignment of goods, one of the staff looked at him, rubbed the back of his neck in wonder, and said, 'I've been working at one job and another for the best part of forty years and this is the first time I've ever seen a boss roll up his sleeves and help.' The boss's actions demonstrated more clearly than words how very important the job was. After that no one ever minded helping out or staying on if it was necessary; they *knew* that their boss spoke the truth.

FALSE PRIDE

How often do we refuse to climb down, admit we are wrong, or refuse to accept criticism because of pride? Being proud of achievement is one thing, but pride that becomes an obstacle to progress or successful negotiation is ridiculous. You may be immensely proud about having found a better way of doing something at work, and then someone comes along who suggests an alternative that could save time. Somehow it feels as if you are being personally attacked when you were enjoying a bit of an ego trip and so you refuse to listen or to apply the new technique.

If you don't have this problem you may still have to work, or live, with people who do. How can you deal with it? One way is to try and present your idea or solution in such a way that they either take it on board believing it to be their own (or partly theirs). You could drop a casual suggestion and leave them to come to their own conclusion that leads to them using your idea. Do not criticize what they are already doing – that is not your aim. Many people will accept a new idea or procedure if they are involved in the discussions, but put up a brick wall if they are told to do it.

There is a distinct difference between pride and arrogance. Arrogance is the ego at work, pride is tempered by humility. People who are justly proud can be delightful; people who use arrogance can be a real pain. Have you ever worked with someone who is always boasting?

AVOIDING PANIC

When the pressure is on and people become stressed, a build-up of energy results which can easily prompt a panic response. When we panic we are unable to think clearly or act in the best way.

Most panic is caused in the workplace by running out of time. Here's how to avoid leaving things until the last minute: list your order of priorities. It's a good piece of advice to do this at the beginning of each day. When you find yourself running out of time you need to ask: How urgent is it? How important is it? Can it wait until tomorrow?

We need to be clear about our priorities. Leaving the most difficult or worst jobs until later doesn't make them go away. Often, doing them first is best. You then have a clear day where you can look forward to the rest of 'things to be done'.

I went once to visit the Managing Director of a large factoring company. He waved his hand at his pending file. 'Do you ever get this happening?' he asked. 'You have a file for things you need to deal with but can't do right now. Perhaps you need time to think about them, or you're waiting for additional information. The next day you flip through the file, some of them once again get pushed on one side. This goes on for a week. Suddenly you realize that the decision has been made for you – it's now too late to do anything about it and you drop the papers in the bin.'

I often think about that man; he had put into words something that ought to be clear but that we so often miss. Things that seem terribly important often turn out to be not that important after all.

Useful tips

Learn to recognize signs of panic and calm down. Breathe deeply for a few minutes and picture a scene that is calm and peaceful. Practice visualizing this when you are sitting on the bus or in the tube train, after supper, and before you go to sleep, so that it is readily available to you when you need it. Also pausing and asking, *What is the worst thing that can happen to me?* will help pull things back into perspective. A panic attack does feel as if some 'unknown' is attacking you and it is hard, at that moment, to see that the real problem lies in the way you are thinking. By

Sometimes we need to ask ourselves does it really matter?

changing your thoughts you give yourself time to calm down. You will then be able to think more clearly. Remember that the worst thing that can happen to you is to die, and that is most unlikely to happen in most situations in the workplace.

WINNING AN ARGUMENT

You have done all the right things. Listened attentively. Given the other person a fair hearing. Focused on the main issue. Taken into account their way of thinking. When things got heated you stepped back, giving each of you a few minutes to collect yourselves. From all the evidence you have you know that you are right and you now point this out. They have no further defence. You win the argument. Do you go away feeling good? Gloat? Sigh with relief and dismiss the whole thing? If you want co-operation in the future, if you want the best outcome, you will need to take the time to make that person feel comfortable about what has happened. Caring about the person and his feelings is vital in a good working relationship; it is also important to your own growth as a human being. Let's see how you could do this.

Imagine that you work for the local education authority and your job is to organize transport for disabled children. You instruct your assistant to inform the parents of new children, for whom you arrange transport, of the dates for half-term. But somehow she confuses your instructions and telephones around to tell them that transport will be available for them *following* the half-term holiday. When this comes to light she explains that this is what you told her to do. You pull out the notes you had left with her and point to the top of the page. Here it is clearly typed when collection is to begin. There is some further discussion. By now she's feeling vulnerable and a little stupid. The error has to be corrected. You can now throw the papers back at her and tell her to phone everyone concerned and explain her mistake thereby leaving her to cope with her embarrassment. Or you help find a way out for her. Reason tells you the mistake wasn't intentional, she was trying to do her best and to follow instructions. Unfortunately she got these wrong. However, gloating over her predicament or feeling a sense of satisfaction because you were right, isn't going to improve your working relationship. Neither do you want her to spend the next few days feeling bad about it. 'Look here,' you say, 'it isn't the end of the world. I've made mistakes myself, it can happen to anyone. I know you'll be extra careful following instructions next time. Just apologize for the error – no need to say it was yours.'

UNDERSTANDING

Most of what I have covered in this chapter so far deals with interaction between management, authorities and staff, but much conflict can occur between people sharing the same work. If you are experiencing negative behaviour with co-workers try to understand the way they think. Find out what they are feeling, whether they are really getting at you because they cannot attack the person directly concerned. If, for example, a woman is having trouble at home, she may come to work and take it out on someone who either cannot retaliate or isn't important to her. She may be using you without realizing it. You could help by deliberately choosing to take your tea break at the same time and approaching her. Perhaps you start by saying, 'I'm sorry you feel so upset' – this doesn't admit that the fault is yours – 'but you seem so unhappy and I wondered if it's more than the photocopier (or whatever caused the dispute) that's troubling you. Can I help in any way?' By using this approach you are giving her an opening; she no longer has the need to protect herself, and you may be able to help. You have opened the way to being her friend instead of her enemy.

In some problem areas you may need to examine the other person's way of thinking. Do this with an open mind and you will sometimes discover that their way of thinking is better than yours. You can then learn from it, implement their suggestions, or adopt their ideas. We can learn so much from each other once we move beyond the need to defend ourselves and to protect our egos.

Where there is a difference of opinion, unfair criticism, or people who refuse to listen, try to avoid buying into negative emotions. Don't turn the situation around so that you only consider its affects upon you. It is far more productive to stay positive and investigate *why* a certain situation has arisen. Dealing with the cause rather than the effect means getting to the root of the problem.

Suppose a colleague flatly refuses to take over the work you have been doing on the computer, saying: 'You started it, you finish it. It's not my responsibility!' But you have other work to complete before going home and she has nothing important to do. You may choose to interpret this reaction as selfish, or that she thinks your work inferior and doesn't want to get involved, or that she is being deliberately awkward. Or you may ask: 'Can you help me to understand what the problem is?' You then discover she is terrified of messing things up and has never actually used that program before. She may be scared of looking foolish in your eyes, or her own.

EXCLUSION

How do you respond when you discover that you have been excluded from a function that involves everyone else in the office? (This also applies to gatherings involving families and friends.) It could be an outing, a wedding, a fiftieth birthday celebration, a christening, an evening at the bowling alley. Do you feel deliberately ignored, rejected, undervalued, snubbed, disliked? Treatment like this can really hurt or knock your confidence for six. You could ask why or assume the worst – that they really don't want your company; or you could let it pass and see it as not being that important. Tim, who is an office manager, discovered that the rest of the people in his office had been invited to the evening celebration of one of the girls who was getting married. Although he didn't actively enquire if everyone was going, it looked that way. He shrugged, after all he didn't know the girl very well and it was hardly likely to ruin his life if he didn't get invited. A few days before the wedding she came to his desk and asked if he had made a decision yet. She was actually feeling hurt that he was the only one in the office who hadn't accepted her invitation. 'But I never received one,' he explained. It turned out that she had quietly slipped it into his In-tray without saying anything and he had missed it.

How often we jump to conclusions without knowing all the facts. If you are upset over a situation that involves others, before leaping to defend yourself (or to attack), ask yourself, *Do I have all the facts?* This way you can avoid many upsets and confrontations. Many people 'hear' and then go off and make their own interpretation based on what they *thought* they heard. This is biased thinking and can be very negative.

Where money or space is involved we do have to decide where invitations stop. If you are not invited and you feel good about yourself, exclusion ought not to bother you – you should be able to appreciate the situation. This also applies to things like birthday and Christmas gifts, awards and treats. One shop assistant whose daughter was getting married explained the situation to her colleague: 'We would love to invite you but we have had to decide on a budget now that Jeff's retired . . .' There wasn't any need to say more, her words conveyed the message that she cared and trusted that her friend would understand.

MISTAKES DO HAPPEN

Everyone makes mistakes some of the time, at work this can be very serious. Before exploding at the person responsible it is imperative to ask yourself: was this done intentionally? If it wasn't, bawling someone out is only going to make them feel even worse and will do nothing to rectify the situation.

People don't deliberately make mistakes, but all too often we rush to attack them for their foolishness, carelessness, ignorance, incompetence. Getting angry, upset, accusing them, can make things even worse, for when someone becomes intimidated they find it harder to think clearly or to function properly. Keeping your cool and communicating clearly is a far better way of improving matters.

The self-righteous prig who declares he never makes mistakes is deluding himself and preventing himself from seeing how, when a mistake does happen, all is not lost if it is used as a learning experience.

Some people are so insecure that they are afraid to admit that they could possibly make a mistake or do anything wrong and will search around for someone else to blame. This can make them look ridiculous and lose the respect of others. If you are in the line of fire, and the accusation thrust at you is unjust, refuse to accept the blame, send it back from whence it came. When, for example, papers you have been accused of losing are discovered in the boss's briefcase, he may still try to offload the mistake on to some other innocent being. This kind of delusionary behaviour is frequently prompted by fear: the self-esteem of these kind of people is so fragile they cannot cope with being wrong. Perhaps if you work or live with someone like this you can exercise a little compassion and help them to focus on their achievements and successes. Later smirking and declaring 'I told you so!' won't improve the situation.

Roger works as an electronics engineer. He is extremely clever but fails to pay attention to small detail. A new design is sent to a potential customer with one important detail missing. Roger believes that he never makes mistakes and accuses his secretary: she should have picked it up. But she isn't the engineer and although she picks up errors in dictation she doesn't have the knowledge to recognize this kind of omission. 'I'm sorry, Roger, but you couldn't have told me, or expected me to do it. I don't know anything about digital electronics. With your workload though, I'm not surprised that it should happen, you have so much to think about.' Here we see that although she has refused to accept responsibility for his mistake, she helps him to recover his self-esteem by suggesting why he forgot to include the detail. It was kind and thoughtful of her, it cost little, and their good working relationship is maintained.

If you have made a mistake, acknowledge it and take action to rectify it. When you are in the wrong it doesn't hurt to apologize.

ANOTHER LOOK AT SELF-TALK

We can use internal dialogue to build our confidence, to change a behaviour or to reframe an attitude. Or we can use self-talk to destroy our self-image, render us helpless or create negative attitudes. Either way, we may be completely unaware that we are doing this.

Silent muttered words, or negative self-talk has a subliminal effect. It's a bit like the days when messages were flickered on to the cinema screen; one wasn't even able to read them at a conscious level so that they bypassed the logical mind and went straight to the unconscious part of the brain. In this way the cinema-goer was prompted to go into the foyer and purchase food and drinks without being consciously aware of why he had made the decision to do so.

If you are thinking negative or derogatory things, they are going to influence the way you see yourself and others. *Stupid imbecile! Idiot! Can't you ever get anything right? What makes you think anyone is going to listen to you?* When words like this are directed towards yourself, or another, they can all too easily cause conflict and create self-doubt and also affect the way you interact with others. Life will feel a lot better when you learn to catch yourself doing this and make a deliberate effort to *stop doing it*.

Do not generalize, not everything you do, or someone else does, is a waste of time, stupid and idiotic. Look for the good in yourself and others and remember that, when you expect people to respond positively, most do.

SUCCESSFUL NEGOTIATION

To successfully negotiate you must be sure of your facts. If you have to retract you will send out the message that you don't really know what you are talking about and people will no longer trust your judgement or be convinced by your arguments. Try to see both points of view. Understand the thinking processes of the other person.

Keep discussions impersonal if possible. Where you have to criticize, remember that people do tend to take criticism personally, therefore direct any necessary criticism at the deed, act or problem, *not* the person. Don't drag up old issues. The way you influence others will depend upon the message behind your words and the way you communicate this. There may be areas where you will have to agree to disagree and, if you are in a position of authority, may need to insist on a certain procedure even though the other person does not see things your way: 'Yes, I understand why you feel it is quicker in this case to handwrite the lists but I still need them to be put into the computer, please.' Beware of *having* to be right, it has no place in successful negotiation, the important thing is to do what is best.

When you wish someone to do something and you are aware that there is going to be resistance, a more effective way is to offer ideas indirectly by suggestion. To do this it is essential to know the other person. If you talk in a way that assumes he believes the things that he does not believe, you are influencing by suggestion. Establish rapport and then offer the ideas indirectly and the other person accepts them automatically. To do this you need to start with ideas that are easily acceptable and then progress to your objective: you talk around the subject rather than analysing it. Let's see how it might work:

You wish to move one of your staff into another department. This lady is skilled but rather shy and resistant to change – it makes her feel threatened and unsafe. You have already mentioned the need for someone to move, now you say: 'Jane, you've been doing a wonderful job here. I can see how you have grasped the essentials and appreciate how your skills could be used to benefit both the firm and yourself when you move on to Department X. They urgently need someone like you. There is a very friendly atmosphere in that department and you will be left to get on with your work in your own way. I've asked the department head to introduce you to the work team and Jackie is looking forward to having you with them. I wonder if you could show them how to use the new FR2 equipment. I've arranged for your desk to be taken over there tomorrow.' You haven't scared her by focusing on the change this will involve, neither have you discussed how it will directly affect her, but you have made her feel that she is needed and that you have absolute confidence in her ability so that she will not feel threatened. You also spoke as if this is about to happen and not something under debate. Arranging for her desk to go with her means she won't feel completely cut-off from the environment where she has come to feel safe.

All this manoeuvring may seem a waste of time – why can't people just do as they are asked? However, it is worth the effort and will lead to greater efficiency. People who are happy in their environment work well and produce less mistakes. They also send out positive energy from which we can all benefit.

EXPECTATION

There is a lovely story of a woman who opened the door to a man she believed was the plumber. She had a tap that wouldn't turn off and it needed a new washer. Her husband had recently died and, until his death, he had always dealt with these kinds of jobs in the home himself. Before the man had a chance to speak she escorted him to the bathroom and gave him her husband's tool box. The man changed the washer and assured her it would not cause her any more trouble. When asked how much she owed him he shook his head and said there wasn't any charge, it had only taken him five minutes. He was actually a sales representative who had been sent cold-calling to try and generate some business for a double-glazing window firm. 'Why didn't you tell her?' his wife asked him, when he later related the story. 'I couldn't,' he replied. 'What she needed right then was for someone to stop the tap from dripping and I could see that it wasn't the moment to try and sell her double glazing.' Isn't it amazing what expectation will do?

Expectation affects results. It is a positive energy that influences everyone around. However, if the expectation is unrealistic it can create despondency and people end up feeling pressurized or bullied. Where management expects five workers to accomplish the same amount of work that eight used to do – and we hear more and more of this as people try to cut back on spending – they will not get better results. People feel used, exploited, unappreciated. They also get over-burdened and tired.

Discovering that you can do more, or expand your thinking, or use your skills in ways you have never dreamed of, can be a wonderful revelation and leads to a good sense of self-worth. Like the supervisor in the clothes shop who started as a counter assistant and told me, 'I never dreamt I could ever supervise until management suggested I give it a try.' Many people fail to realize their potential because of poor personal expectations.

There is nothing wrong with having goals, but some of the time we need to make haste slowly. Expectations are fine so long as they are realistic. When people understand *why* more is expected of them, they are far more willing to make that extra effort. If you are an employee and feel that you are in this situation, ask. This will show that you are interested in the success of the firm. Who knows, it could lead to promotion!

FACE TO FACE CONFLICT

When the problem is directly yours, stick to the point and express this clearly. If you think you are being unfairly treated, or asked to do things which are not in your job specification, explain why you feel you cannot do them. If others seem to be getting preferential treatment: working fewer hours, being given travelling expenses or protective clothing, you have the right to ask why this is so.

Where colleagues are clearly not pulling their weight and more of the burden is falling on you, first talk to them about it – perhaps they are not aware of what is happening. Should this fail to resolve the situation you may have to speak to your immediate boss. Once he has been made aware he should take action that does not rebound on you. Many people put up with a lot for fear of reprisals – this shouldn't happen if everyone is open and explanations have already been given as to why certain things need to change or to be done differently.

Some people believe that certain jobs are beneath them; if they are employed to do secretarial work they do not believe they should be asked to make the tea, post the mail, work in reception. The sad thing is that these people usually have a poor sense of self-worth and need the image their job allows in order to function. I know of a boss in a small firm who used to clean out the toilets himself because his staff thought it was degrading to do such a chore. In cases like this it can happen that willing staff are taken advantage of by others and do far more than is fair.

In the workplace things are seen from two points of view: the boss's and the staff's.

In attempting to resolve a conflict, unfair accusations will achieve nothing, unwillingness to co-operate will slow things down and things considered unreasonable will be sabotaged or will not be implemented.

It is, therefore, essential for all concerned that a point of reference is established:

1   decide what the problem is
2   establish the desired outcome
3   determine the best way of making this come about.

Although unions in most cases do much good in representing and caring for their members, strikes and picketing still happen and can incite fear, conflict, and direct confrontation. How do you keep control of a group determined to cause trouble? We have to remember that however unreasonable someone else's point of view may appear, they have the right to their own opinion. People who feel very strongly about something find it hard to listen to any alternative. If you belong to a union but do not support their views you might still be expected to back their actions. When you don't, it could be seen as betrayal. This doesn't mean you don't have the right to follow your conscience but you are likely to suffer reprisals – colleagues will often resort to childish, petty behaviour. By remaining courteous and firm you will avoid at least some of the reactions of those who view your stand as unacceptable.

A postman I know described how, because he didn't support strike action (he thought it achieved nothing but bad feelings), the mail he sorted was strewn over the floor causing him considerable delay as he had to sort it all over again. We may ask how grown men, many married and with families, could act in this way? The answer has to be that they haven't yet found a more mature way of dealing with those who do not agree with them. To show how they feel they may refuse to speak or to sit with the offender during breaks. So much for democracy and the freedom to follow your own beliefs! Depending on your type of employment, confrontation may occasionally arise and you may be forced into making hard decisions. You have to be very strong to go against the crowd. If they will listen, talking persuasively works better than the 'you are all idiots' approach.

AVOIDING VIOLENCE

Confrontation that is heading towards violence needs immediate action the moment it is recognized. Move back, or move away, perhaps go and make a cup of tea. If you have been opposing certain action but can be seen by others to be genuinely trying to meet them halfway, they may be more open to listening to your view. Another way to stop a tirade of words or abuse is by asking a question. So long as it is a meaningful one your opponents are, we hope, going to pause and consider it; they may then still try to convince you by answering it from their viewpoint, but you will have gained time thus allowing the build up of angry energy to dissipate.

Another way of diffusing violent confrontation is to repeat what is argued by expressing it in your own words: 'Wait a minute, have I got it right. Is this what you mean?' This gives the message that you are listening and trying to understand. You then rephrase the cause of the problem. If all this fails, remove yourself from the scene, you will gain nothing by becoming involved in physical violence. Getting your jaw broken will not solve the problem. Perhaps later, when all parties have calmed down, you can approach the topic again more rationally.

7 Conflict with Strangers

It sounds ridiculous that we can get upset with people we don't even know, those who mean nothing to us and whose opinion of us really ought not to count. But the reality is that conflict with strangers can become so intense that some people will seek to physically damage and even kill in the heat of conflicting emotions.

ROAD RAGE

I have in front of me a newspaper report recounting the story of a taxi-driver who caused the death of a cyclist in a 'road rage' incident and now faces a jail sentence. In his defence the taxi-driver explained his behaviour by saying that the cyclist 'cut him up' and then acted like a madman in the ensuing argument. Another report tells of a man who swerved violently, deliberately hitting another man, whom he then left dying on the pavement from head injuries.

How can such terrible things be avoided? What is going on? Road rage was virtually unheard of ten years ago. On the surface it looks as if people have lost the ability to control their emotions, lack self-discipline, no longer respect others or life and do not consider the consequences of their actions. But something more is going on. Most road rage is a consequence of believing that someone else is not giving you the consideration to which you believe you have the right. This leads us back to the way we are taught and our upbringing. The desire to retaliate is fuelled by the thought, *How dare he do that to me!*

Many people who normally behave calmly seem to change when they get behind the steering wheel. They experience power. In a way the vehicle compensates for personal inadequacies.

If you have been brought up to feel loved, special, that you are important, then you do not have to protect your self-image, bolster your ego, or prove things to complete strangers.

In direct confrontation, admitting you were at fault to someone who is in a rage seems, in their eyes, to justify their anger. They believe they have every right to yell abuse or hit out at you – it was your fault. So you have to move carefully. Even the most reasonable of people have been known to behave irresponsibly when their cars or lives are threatened. A reason for this is rooted in fear that moves the body directly into its survival mode. Blood pressure increases, adrenalin flows in abundance, the body begins to sweat, tension builds up in the muscles and so on. The immediate response to this is to run or fight. It is part of the animal world and we would do well to remind ourselves that we also are animals with the same instincts for survival. By pausing for a few moments before reacting, the logical civilized response is restored and, although perhaps your car is written off causing great inconvenience, you are still alive.

Road rage has become such a serious problem that we all need to learn how to respond should this happen to us. Behaviour strategies, communication skills, and the right approach can be critical to our well-being.

Most of the time when there is a road accident or incident, both parties believe that it was not their fault. By accusing the other person for the bad driving incident we protect our own position and believe we are justified in being upset or angry.

A car, to many, is a status symbol. It may seem more important to them than their own life, and when an accident or incident happens, all the driver's energy is directed towards protecting this symbol of prestige. It has been suggested that one reason most road incidents are caused by men is, to some extent, due to testosterone and how it prompts survival through aggression in males. However, if this were the case, why don't all men get mad when placed in a threatening situation? And here we are, back to lessons taught in the home – it is essential that we learn, and teach our young, self-discipline and respect for others. Self-discipline and respect are the core of civilization.

My friend Fred and I turned a corner in the High Street to see traffic congestion which had brought everything to a halt. One lady driver, who needed to back into the only available space in order to allow a large lorry to pass, seemed incapable of reversing her car. A man who had just stepped out of his van began to shout obscenities at her. The woman looked confused and very red in the face.

Fred stepped forward. 'Just a moment,' he said to the yelling man, 'that lady is doing her best, she can't help being a poor driver.'

'Then she shouldn't be on the road!' the man declared angrily.

Fred looked the man in the eye and told him, 'I happen to know she has a bad heart and looks after an elderly sick mother at home. She's under a lot of stress.'

'That's her problem, not mine!' The van driver thumped the back of her car and returned to his swearing.

Fred intervened again. 'Try being gentle with her. Perhaps she doesn't realize she can reverse into that space.' (It had a NO PARKING sign beside it.)

Not getting anywhere with the lady driver the man now directed all his pent-up frustration on to Fred. 'Do you want me to thump you?' he yelled.

'I shouldn't try if I were you,' Fred said. (He's six foot tall and heftily built.)

'See my dog?' The man pointed to a large Alsatian sitting in the front seat. 'I could let him out on you.'

At this point I moved away into the bookshop I had come to visit and left them to it.

A few minutes later Fred joined me, smiling, 'All sorted out,' he said, and turned to look at the books.

We were talking to the shop owner some ten minutes later when the door was flung open and the angry van driver came in.

'So this is where you are!' he said.

I must admit I felt my own heart thump quite violently at this point. We all turned to look at the man.

'I knew I'd find you,' he declared. 'I just came back to say I was in the wrong. I should never have spoken to that woman the way I did. The truth is I'm all wound up; I'm waiting to have a liver operation.'

We expressed sympathy and I told him how I admired his courage in coming back to apologize.

'Well, I was in the wrong,' he said. Then, turning to the shop owner, he asked, 'You don't happen to have a book on *How To Do Your Own Liver Transplant*, do you?'

This made us all laugh and we spent fifteen minutes chatting comfortably together.

This true story beautifully demonstrates how the right approach can diffuse an explosive situation and how, if we better understood people and perhaps learned to be a little more charitable, many conflicts could be averted.

Confident people, not needing to prove anything to themselves or others, do not take the bad driving behaviour of others personally. They see it as either an error of judgment (and we can all make those), a thoughtless moment (we all have those too), something going wrong with the car, or an ill-mannered person who isn't worth getting upset over.

When people are stressed they often react violently where normally they would never do so. It is worth looking for the reason why someone reacts so forcefully before getting into a heated argument. There are medical reasons why some people become very upset in tense or threatening situations. Again they may not even be aware that they have, for example, an over-active thyroid, diabetes, an incubating virus, or a brain tumour.

STRATEGIES THAT WORK

When someone verbally attacks you and you have no idea why, try asking: 'Did I do something wrong? Is there a problem? Could you explain?' This way you are giving the person thinking time which may be all they need in order to calm down. We can all be thoughtless at times. We may be preoccupied with thoughts of an appointment and are already late, or we may be very worried over a relative who is ill. Bear this in mind when next you get into what seems like unwarranted confrontation. When you are in the wrong, if you apologize and explain, this will almost always diffuse a situation.

I was once driving down a steep hill when my car brakes failed. Ahead of me was a parked van, coming up the hill was a car. I pulled on the handbrake but still managed to skid into the side of this new car coming towards me. At the sound of the impact the

If you apologize this will almost always diffuse a situation

van owner came rushing out of the house. The other man leapt from his car and the two of them began shouting at each other. The van driver was convinced the fault was that of the other man who, he believed, should have stopped. The car driver was yelling that if the man hadn't parked his vehicle right on the curve in the road the accident wouldn't have happened. All this time I was standing alongside them trying to get in a word. 'But it was my fault,' I repeated. 'My brakes failed.' After a few minutes I actually got through to them and they both paused, looked at me for a moment and then returned to verbally attacking each other again. They both refused to change their direction of thinking and acknowledge they had made a mistake – as far as they were each concerned the fault lay with the other man. It really was funny; even at the time I can remember thinking how ridiculous the whole situation had become. Of course it was eventually sorted out, but this goes to show how we need to take a few moments to think about a situation before jumping to conclusions.

However, changing direction is hard for most people, especially when they lack confidence. We do sometimes need to review our approach or ideas about certain things and changing your mind can result in new insight or a good experience. The thought, for example, that all bank managers are only after your money and charge extortionate fees, may be completely reversed when one goes out of his way to help you start a new business, or gives his free time to see you after working hours.

Muttering what a thoughtless rude idiot the woman is who just pushed in front of you can prompt a very nasty reaction. If you want to say something and really believe it is essential, say it directly to the person concerned.

The best learned lessons, as we know, are from example. You have to be seen backing up your words with action for them to carry any real impact.

Getting mad with the telephone man because your line is temporarily out of order won't put the matter right any faster. In fact, while you go on at him you're preventing him from getting on with his job. And is it his fault personally that things have gone wrong? Often when we attack a person verbally we are really frustrated with the system, angry because the product has let us down or disappointed us, or the service we have come to expect has failed us.

We make our demands depending on how these things affect us. Attacking the girl who sold you a shirt because the buttons fell off isn't going to put things right. She may not have the authority to replace it without first speaking to her boss. By being courteous and understanding of her position you may be sure that she will do everything possible to find a satisfactory solution.

When people abuse you, misuse you, 'take you for a ride', or let you down, you become disillusioned and distrust creeps in. Giving people the benefit of the doubt before accusing or attacking is by far the best approach. If you have had many bad experiences you may tend to focus on those instead of all the occasions when people have treated you fairly, and the product or service you purchased was excellent. Those who have become out-and-out cynics fail to recognize anyone as being genuine and lead an isolated miserable life.

Where health is concerned we do, at times, become extremely anxious, especially if we feel helpless in the hands of our doctor or hospital staff. Afraid of reprisals, the patient struggles to co-operate when often feeling that the diagnosis, treatment, or refusal to consider the illness from a different angle threatens his future. If this happens to you or your loved ones, remember what is at stake and speak firmly to someone – you may even have to clearly state that you will take things further if you do not get the help you seek. However, gentle persuasion usually achieves far more. No one wants conflict at such worrying times, but if, for example, you believe your child isn't getting better and needs a second opinion, ask for it. This applies in many areas of life where we feel at the mercy of strangers. If you are normally a retiring sort of person who finds it difficult to speak up, ask someone close for their support. I recall an elderly lady whom I knew who was having a terrible time with false teeth that didn't fit. The dentist had told her there was nothing wrong and that her problem was psychological. I accompanied her to the dental hospital and with my support she felt confident enough to insist on seeing an expert. The outcome was that he recognized her gums could not support the dental plate and a more sophisticated design was needed. This made the difference between spending the rest of her days indoors (she hated being seen without teeth), or having the freedom to enjoy the last years of her life shopping and visiting friends. All this was achieved without using anger but by being firm and refusing to accept that nothing could be done.

I also suggest that you stay alert for lip service that is often used to placate but leaves things unchanged. There is a belief in some businesses that if you soft-talk the customer you put them off taking further action and that most people will then stop pestering. Isn't it true how we sometimes do this? It happened to Joan when she had the end part of her house re-tiled. A few weeks later she noticed that one tile had slipped. After making three phone calls and getting nowhere she gave up: 'I can't keep going on at them,' she said. Now her son is going to do it for her.

Of course we don't actively seek out confrontation, but when it is the only way, make sure that you stay in control. If people are trying to put you down or intimidate you (perhaps by using their knowledge or position of authority) using this visualization technique will help.

Exercise 5 – Protecting yourself in a volatile situation

1   Stop speaking for a moment – no matter what's going on – take a couple of really deep breaths, and as you do this imagine a protective barrier around you. This can be anything that comes easily to mind, an electric field, a suit of armour. (I had one woman who used to imagine herself wrapped up in foil.) This visualization changes your focus and removes your mind from perceiving yourself as the victim.

2   Now, if you want to take control of the conversation, visualize an outgoing force such as a rocket, aeroplane, or

express train. Picture it going away from you. This moves you out of the receptive mode and into the outgoing mode.

3 You are now ready to express your views, give an explanation if necessary, and bring the argument to a satisfactory conclusion.

Using this exercise really does help. Emotions do often get in the way, preventing us from expressing ourselves clearly. If you are with a very forceful person you may be afraid of bursting into tears. Using positive visualization enables you to calm down. You then move from coping with the situation to controlling it.

Powerful emotions sometimes result in 'close-down'. We switch off, and by not thinking we deny our feelings. This can be very dangerous. On the one hand we become vulnerable; on the other, when we lose touch with our feelings, it is possible to cause material damage, an act of violence, or even commit murder.

Have you sometimes wondered how people can do the terrible things that you hear about? It is often because, at that time, they have lost contact with their inner self where values are seated. If you stop feeling in battle, it enables you to shoot the enemy, whereas if, at that moment, you related to the enemy as another human being, you would most likely be unable to pull the trigger.

In some cases the unreal becomes real and people behave as if the imagined act has been done or the situation actually exists. This can be funny, as in the case of the man who came home and found his wife locked in the bathroom. She explained that there was a mouse in the house and it had chased her upstairs. This belief was so strong that she had been in the bathroom for several hours awaiting his return. Of course mice do not chase people, but in her mind they did.

A friend of mine, when she reads a fiction story, becomes so involved that she experiences being part of the plot. She remarked one day to her husband, 'I haven't been able to get dinner ready, this man is about to be shot if anyone moves.' We all transport ourselves into fantasy land some of the time, it can be fun and is relaxing, but we need to know how to release ourselves from those internal pictures and return to reality. For those who fail to do this, terrible things can happen. Prompted by pictures of violence and rape they go out and do something similar. In such situations it is almost impossible to reach the mind of that person, you become part of his fantasy. The same thing can also happen to people who take certain drugs. You may be an innocent stranger but someone's psychotic behaviour can still affect you. Where needless violence or vandalism is happening, the safest course of action is to call the police.

However, if someone else's life is at stake you may feel compelled to act. Using words without accusing may work: 'Look, he's only a frail old man,' or 'She's just a little girl.' Or you may try a request: 'Please, don't do that.' If you can get people talking you distract the mind and stand a better chance of bringing them back to reality: 'You must be very angry, or upset . . . ' Leave it open, if they need to talk you have opened a door.

VANDALISM

This is another cancer of modern society that creates feelings of anger and despair. Often, acts of vandalism are thoughtless, we don't know who did them, and there seems nothing we can do to stop them. Wrong! We can! We need to remove the cloak of complacency which protects us and get involved with police initiatives to reduce such crimes, join Neighbourhood Watch, support political decisions that are made to eradicate vandalism, educate our children to respect other people's property.

We hear so much criticism of the police these days that we forget their job is to protect us. Instead of looking for the isolated cases where there is error or incorrect procedure we should keep our minds on the overall good of our police force and support them. If you speak in derogatory terms about the police in front of your children they will get the message that they are the enemy or people to be scorned. What a child needs is to trust the police – one day her life may depend on it.

Over and over again we read of people attempting to explain – even justify – unruly behaviour, violence and vandalism, theft and even rape. Many now suggest that such behaviour is due to one-parent families, poor housing conditions, unemployment. The most recent survey indicates that it is because fathers have to work such long hours and see little of their children. Well, these situations existed before World War Two, during the war, and afterwards, but we did not have the crimes that are now still escalating. During my own childhood, (I was five when the war started) no child was afraid to walk alone either in the daylight or at night. I recall how we would go across the fields picking blackberries and Mother would send the dog with a note in his collar to find us when tea was ready.

I have spoken with many people who recall those pre- and post-war times and without exception they agree that murder, street rape, vandalism and violation of the laws were so rare they found it difficult to recall one case. They rarely locked doors, would always stop and help someone in trouble or whose car had broken down, and the only kind of drugs they knew about were the ones their doctor might prescribe. They agreed that what had changed was the degree of discipline and respect for other people and their property. Civilization as we knew it is on the way out, *unless we take action now*. It is not a bad thing to report a wrong-doer, caught early enough it may still be possible to direct their energies into other positive actions.

TERRITORIAL RIGHTS

The natural part of our primitive urge to survive has now evolved to cover all manner of things that are, in reality, no longer necessary to survival. We seem to have lost our way. We live with the misguided belief that we need to have more and more material possessions. We then go on to protect these, often with our lives, as we live with the illusion that they are essential to us. In some communities everything is still shared, but for most modern day men and women the unfortunate belief is, 'what is mine is mine' and look out if you step over that invisible line of demarcation!

A tremendous amount of conflict is caused by people believing that others have no right to own or to do certain things. They wish to protect their privacy, their 'space' – even when they don't actually own it. They see foreigners who wish to settle nearby as a threat, or they don't want a youth club by them, or they don't want the local pub to play music on Friday nights.

Ethnic divisions are causing unrest and even erupting into violence with people wanting their own schools and religious places of worship where they can follow their own faith. Recognizing the rights of small groups, homosexuals, racial minorities, the underprivileged, has not resolved the problem. What does seem to be needed is a deeper understanding and respect for each other and healthy integration.

Of course people's misuse and abuse of land and property is wrong, and people are right to try and protect the environment, to prevent pollution, and to stop the discharge of harmful substances into rivers and seas that are a threat to health and life. But surely there are ways to influence decisions and the actions of those who have the power to make or change the laws without setting fire to ships, overturning lorries, vandalizing builder's equipment, invading the premises of research laboratories?

Protection of our way of life, and the Earth we inhabit, should be achieved with reverence and responsibility. Resorting to childish acts of destruction or opposition does not build a healthy future for our children. The fact that we must now all lock our doors, be careful to avoid going out at night alone, carry mobile telephones as a safety precaution, surely tells us that what we are currently doing will not resolve the problems, neither will it alleviate conflict.

It is also important that we avoid making such sweeping statements as: all Blacks are ignorant, all Germans are arrogant, all politicians should be shot, never trust an Irishman, teachers are idiots. We know this isn't true, and yet so many people go on saying these kind of things. I watched a live American show the other day where a number of volunteers from the audience were being questioned about their attitude towards Black people. One woman stated that she truly believed all Black people were the same and that she could never like one. A number of Black people then volunteered to go into another room and talk with her – when she came back she had changed her view. *That was all it took.*

RECOGNIZING THE DANGER SIGNS

Certain things happen before people become explosive. Learning to recognize the signs early on means we can usually prevent physical violence. Here are some of them: the voice tone changes, hands are made into fists or they begin to make threatening gestures, deep breathing replaces normal breaths, pupils dilate, the face becomes red, the body stance becomes aggressive.

When you recognize the other person is losing control:

- Avoid direct accusations.
- Do not become verbally abusive.
- Use words that indicate you are listening to what the person has to say – this can be achieved by re-wording statements that reflect the problem.
- Step back. Acknowledge that you are both upset and ask how best the person thinks you could sort this out e.g. exchange insurer's names, find out more about the situation, use a mediator.
- Agree to differ. If your thinking processes are very different there may be no way of reconciliation.

When you are losing control:

- Be aware of internal self-justification.
- Ask yourself if it is really worth getting this upset.

- Listen to the other person's point of view and try to understand why he or she is so upset.
- Recognize your own resistance and other influential forces (e.g. my husband will go berserk when I tell him).
- Acknowledge other external forces that may be preventing you from thinking straight (e.g. your wife is just about to have a baby and this idiot has run into the side of your car).
- Do not use threats. Recognize your own desire to retaliate.
- Focus on how to resolve the problem.

When you use reactive behaviour it means that you are out of control. You need to know how to detach yourself from unproductive emotions; to do this ask yourself what you will achieve by feeling that way. Does it help you to think more clearly or to state your case in a way that can be understood? Is it going to help you find a satisfactory solution?

There is a big difference between being aggressive and being assertive. Of course it isn't right to let other people always put you down, get away with things, or accuse you unjustly. Allowing this does nothing for your self-esteem, it also indicates to the other person that such behaviour is permissible which doesn't do the aggressor or anyone else any long-term good. Remember that when you choose to back off you have maintained control, *you made a choice*.

People who react are often insecure and inwardly afraid – they cannot afford to be wrong – being unable to cope with what they perceive as failure. The ego raises its head crying, *I can't let him get away with that!* Aggression may demonstrate itself through verbal abuse and angry accusations, physical acts of violence or destruction, or thoughts that fuel further anger and self-justification.

You need to feel confident enough to be assertive when that is the right course of action to take, but it does take courage. Remember your body language counts so try to avoid a threatening stance. Address the problem rather than the person. 'You imbecile, cutting down that tree!' is not the best way to prevent

There is a big difference between being aggressive and being assertive

further devastation to the trees that edge the car-park. Try to talk about the tree not the person's action: 'Excuse me, but I'm sure you can't be aware that there is a tree preservation order to protect our environment.' The man explains that he's just doing his job. You can then go on to explain, if you choose, that trees are being cut down at the rate of an acre per minute. We hope, at this stage, he will volunteer to pass on the information to the management. If, however, you are met with belligerence and total lack of co-operation you can explain that because it is so important you will have to take further action. Then make it clear that you don't really want to take things that far. Try to get his co-operation. Breathe evenly, speak calmly, offer him a chance to back down without losing face. What you have done here is to use a good recipe for constructive assertive behaviour that stands the best chance of success.

- You avoided accusing him directly or suggesting he should have known better.
- You stated your interest.
- You gave concrete reasons.
- You listened to him, openly recognizing his position.
- You suggested a solution.
- You remained respectful.

Let's end the conflict and find a solution.

8   *Living In Harmony*

I hope that what I have shared with you in the previous chapters will help lead you to a holistic caring approach for all life. As Albert Schweitzer discovered, unless he developed a reverence for all living things, his life was bereft of purpose and meaning.

Beware of your ego. Notice where you react when you ought to respond. Reactive behaviour is an indicator that you are out of control just as reactive conditions on Earth are an indicator that Earth is out of control.

In our quest for harmony and peace we must stop categorizing and generalizing. Negative thoughts that begin with *all people* are a warning that you – or those using this phrase – are assuming that a race, or collection of people, all behave in the same way, or that they all have the same values, or that they suffer the same faults.

It is dangerous to assume you *know* based on very little information, biased opinions, or other people's say-so. Before being led into actions that are likely to affect others, it is wise to ask yourself, 'Do I know this for a fact?' And, 'Am I acting on my own principles or in response to theirs?'

The way we behave to a large extent is influenced by:

- our needs – we will fight for food, air, attention
- our upbringing and experiences
- the way we view life
- the values we place on ourselves and others

All too often our egos gets in the way of fair, logical thinking. We become arrogant, focusing only on how things effect us and what we can 'get out of it.' We become greedy. The terrible thing is that our ego trips becomes collective and whole nations are led into conflict and war. Believing that you are part of a super race, or that you have the right to certain land, or that your religious beliefs are the only right ones, is both dangerous and foolhardy. We become aggressive and fuel our actions with motives and goals to support the collective ego. We come to believe that we are more important and that we have more rights than other races or nations.

When you ask people to justify such beliefs you are told: we have the right because we are civilized; we educated those people; we have nurtured the savages . . . But does this really give any group of people the right to plunder another country, to take away for gain the natural resources or products of their land?

We should give, educate, feed, heal for the good of mankind, not because of what we stand to gain.

Many seemingly righteous ventures into poor, underdeveloped countries where man attempted to enforce his religious beliefs were truly no more than ego trips. Natives often exchanged their right to think for themselves, to learn and evolve naturally in their own way and in their own time in return for clothing, food, medicine and trinkets.

We are now witnessing the results of our enforcing 'civilization' on others, most noticeably in the violation of land and pollution of water. Where we failed to pass on true values we have, in some cases, now removed ourselves and left the natives of those countries with half-values – wanting what the white man had but not having the experience to follow through and with only half-taught lessons. There are now many who violate their own land and murder their own people in search of those things they believe they need but which, in truth, often do not matter.

Before doing anything that infringes on man's freedom or his rights we would do well to search our hearts and to ask the question: *What is my real intention?* This applies equally to politicians where many are so clearly riding the ego trip. What makes them believe they are so right? Is their intention to achieve what is best for all men and women, or for the party to which they subscribe?

Naturally there are good people in politics who, while acting with true humility, serve the people by following a path which leads to the benefit of all. But I would just like to hear some politicians occasionally listen with courtesy to the 'other side', and to consider with sincerity what is being said. They might learn something. I do not believe destructive dialogue aids their 'cause' and from my conversation with other 'ordinary' people, I know that many are sick of the politicians rude, dirt-throwing, destructive verbal rantings. I would like to ask: 'What truly good things do you plan to achieve?'

At an individual level, no one can make your choices for you, no one can set your goals, no one can motivate you, unless you decide this is what you really want. But if you want to help change the world into a better place, you can.

Visualization and positive affirmation will help you achieve your goals. You can live in peace and harmony with those whose lives touch yours. Learning to care for people you meet on life's path is not self-sacrifice but the way to happiness and world peace.

My recipe would be something like this: *let every thought and action be motivated by love; care for others; respect those with physical and mental disabilities; be truthful and honest; revere all life; honour the Earth.*

The time has come to take a look at what we are doing to Earth and how we can help create positive long-term effect. We are part of the total energy system that is our universe. When one part of an organism fails to function or to fulfil its role the rest suffers. Earth is a living organism where each part contributes towards the whole. Of all the things man is now doing in the name of progress, decimation of the trees is perhaps causing the most immediate harm. We cannot live without vegetation; we cannot live without trees. Not only do we need trees to enable us to breath, they balance Earth.

We have to reconcile global conflict and to assume our true roles as carers of Earth. It can be done. It takes only 17 per cent to move into another mode.

Mother Earth will survive, however, whether we humans will be part of its future will depend on what we do now.

It is possible to create world peace, and your contribution does count. *When your intention is for good every time you say I CAN, every time you say I WILL, every time you say THIS EXPERIENCE COUNTS, every time you say I FORGIVE, you are helping to create a better world.*

Organizations Offering Advice and Support

Using your telephone directory you can find the number to any of the following organizations who are there to help and advise you. If the organization is not listed in your area you can obtain the number of its head office through the telephone operator or your Citizen's Advice Bureau.

AUSTRALIA

Alcohol
Alcohol & Drug Information
   Service
Alcoholics Anonymous

Gambling
Gambling Anonymous
Lifeline

General Counselling
Community Health Centre
Crisis Care
Distress Call
Domestic Violence
Lifeline

HIV & AIDS
AIDS Council

Homosexuality
Gay Counselling Service

Missing Persons
Red Cross
The Salvation Army

Pregnancy
Childbirth Education Association
Pregnancy Support Centre

Rape
Lifeline
Rape Crisis Centre

Young People
Distress Call

CANADA

Alcohol
Alcohol Abuse
Al-Anon
Ala-teen

Drugs
Addition Research Foundation
Narcotics Anonymous

Eating Disorders
Overeaters Anonymous

Gambling
Gamblers Anonymous

General Information for Residents in Canada
The National Clearing House (tel: 1800 2671291) will always put you in touch with an organization who will help with your problem
Contact **Local Crisis Lines** for help and advice with crisis
Any Government Clinic
Institute of Family Therapy
The CLSC Clinic, Quebec, offers a first line contact

HIV & AIDS
AIDS Hotline
National AIDS Clearing House Information

Homosexuality
Lesbian & Youth, Toronto

Pregnancy
Birthright

Rape & Sexual Abuse
Communications and Public Affairs
Contact local Sexual Assault Support Centres

SOUTH AFRICA

General Counselling and Advice
Compassionate Friends
South African Federation for Mental Health

UNITED KINGDOM

Alcohol Abuse
Accept National Services
Alcohol Concern
Families Anon

Bereavement
CRUSE – offers help and support with bereavement

Drug Abuse
Families Anonymous
National Campaign against Solvent Abuse
Release – helps with drug and abortion problems

Eating Disorders
Anorexia & Bulimia Nervosa Association

Education
Advisory Centre on Education

Family Problems
Social Services Department

Gambling
Gambling Anonymous

General Counselling and Advice
Children's Legal Centre (offers
advice on law affecting young
people)
Institute of Family Therapy
National Association of Citizens
  Advice Bureaux (offers help
  and advice on any subject)
Relate
Samaritans
Youth Access

*HIV, AIDS & Sexually
Transmitted Disease*
National AIDS Helpline
Terrence Higgins Trust and Body
  Positive
Look under VD or contact your
local hospital

Homosexuality
Acceptance Helpline for Parents
Parent's Friend

Mental Disorders
MIND

Missing Person
Missing Persons Bureau
The Salvation Army

One Parent Families
Gingerbread
National Stepfamily Association

Pregnancy
British Pregnancy Advisory
  Service
Brook Advisory Centres
(specialists in birth control for
young people)
Family Planning Association

UNITED STATES OF AMERICA

AIDS Action National Hotline
  1800-342-2437
Al-Anon/Alateen 1800-344-2666
Childhelp USA 1800-422-4453
Gay & Lesbian Adolescent Social
  Services 1310-358-8727
National Drug Abuse Hotline
  1800-662-4357
National Eating Disorders
  Association 1918-481-4092
National Sexually Transmitted
  Disease Hotline
  1800-227-8922

General Information
See self-help guides in local
telephone directories

Further Reading

Frankl, Victor, *Man's Search for Meaning*, Hodder, 1994

Galbraith, Kenneth, *The Culture of Contentment*, Houghton Mifflin, 1992

Grant, Wendy, *Are You In Control?* Element Books, 1995

—— *Dare!* Element Books, 1995

—— *13–19* Element Books, 1996

—— *You & Your Dreams*, Eastbrook Publishing, 1995

Gray, John, *Men Are From Mars, Women Are From Venus*, Thorsons, 1993

Heiman, LoPiccolo, *Becoming Orgasmic*, Piatkus, 1988

Howell, Signe, and Willis, Roy, *Societies at Peace*, Routledge, 1988

Kinder, Melvyn, *Mastering Your Moods*, Simon & Schuster, 1994

Larsen, Earnie, *From Anger to Forgiveness*, Ballantine Books, 1992

Peiffer, Vera, *The Duty Trap*, Element Books, 1996

Saionji, Masami, *Infinite Happiness*, Element Books, 1996

Skynner, Rosin and Cleese, John, *Families and How to Survive Them*, Mandarin, 1993

—— *Life and How to Survive It*, Mandarin, 1994

West-Meads, Zelda, *The Trouble With You*, Hodder & Stoughton, 1995

Williams, Angel, *A Family Affair*, 1996